THE
DATING GAME

Davina McCall is one of Britain's best known TV stars thanks to hits like Channels 4's *Streetmate* and ITV's *Don't Try This At Home*. But before stepping in front of the cameras she had an eclectic and colourful mix of other jobs. She dabbled in pop music under the guiding eye of Eric Clapton, worked as a booker for Models One, and ran one of the most exclusive nightclubs of its day, not to mention working as a singing waitress in Paris. Davina got her first break into TV with MTV and her other small screen successes include *The Real Holiday Show, God's Gift* and the award-winning *The Drop Dead Show*, a one-off *Dispatches* special.

She lives happily in London with her boyfriend and their two dogs, and knows a lot about dating.

THE
DATING GAME

Davina McCall

ARROW

Published by Arrow Books in 2000

3 5 7 9 10 8 6 4 2

First published in the United Kingdom in 2000 by Arrow

Arrow Books Limited
The Random House Group Limited
20 Vauxhall Bridge Road, London SW1V 2SA

Random House Australia (Pty) Limited
20 Alfred Street, Milsons Point, Sydney,
New South Wales 2061, Australia

Random House New Zealand Limited
18 Poland Road, Glenfield,
Auckland 10, New Zealand

Random House (Pty) Limited
Endulini, 5a Jubilee Road, Parktown 2193, South Africa

The Random House Group Limited Reg. No. 954009

www.randomhouse.co.uk

A CIP catalogue record for this book
is available from the British Library

Papers used by Random House
are natural, recyclable products made from wood grown in
sustainable forests. The manufacturing processes conform to
the environmental regulations of the country of origin

ISBN 0 09 941017 6

Typeset in Garamond by MATS, Southend-on-Sea, Essex
Printed and bound in Norway by
AIT Trondheim AS

<u>WARNING</u>

**UNSOLICITED ADVICE GIVEN
LIBERALLY IN THE
FOLLOWING PUBLICATION**

Heed at your own peril . . .

I would like to dedicate this book to:

~~Peter~~

~~James~~

~~Jason~~

~~Dave~~

~~Tristan~~

~~Paul~~

~~Steve~~

Matthew

Joke! This book is for you, Matthew. You put the *grrr* into swinger, baby. Thanks for putting up with me.

ACKNOWLEDGEMENTS

Big thanks to all at Random: Kate (good idea), Mark and of course Sue. Amazing, eh? It started with a walk!

Much love and thanks to Vivian and Charlie (doggers). And I mustn't forget Josh.

Oh, and Mum, Dad and my family, my dogs Rosie and Chloe, John 'the Rottweiler' Noel and Polly.

CONTENTS

Author's note

I may seem an odd candidate to write this book. I've had a string of interesting, exciting and sometimes disastrous relationships and one failed marriage.

So what do I know?
I know a lot !!!

This book is just my take on things. An opinion. Quite a strong one at times! So you might not agree with everything I say – but I hope you'll enjoy it.

I find the whole relationships thing gripping: why do some work when others don't, and how come some of the most successful, gorgeous, charismatic women in the world can't find a man? And some of the most delicious men I know are stuck being single?

What's up with that ???

Well, I've got some far-flung ideas on how to be a **go-getter** and **all woman**. And on the best ways for all you **delicious** men to deal with us. Let me know if they work for you. I'm giving them a trial run myself and **I'm having the time of my life.**

Davina xx

PS. Some of this book is quite serious. Sorry.

Dancing in the Love Desert

OR

The Dilemma

MIDNIGHT AT THE OASIS

♂ ♀	Boy meets girl.
♀ ♂	Girl meets boy.
☺ ♀ ☹	Boy meets 'just someone' and leaves girl.
♀ ♀ ♀ ♀	Girl goes and tells her friends about it. Realises it's for the better.
♂	Boy realises he's made a mistake and wants her back.
♂ ♀	Girl takes him back.
♂ ♀ ♂	Girl runs off with ski instructor two months later.

The course of true love is full of pot holes. Diversions that make you late for romance. And then there's Rush Hour, that tell-tale flood of blood to the cheeks when you spy someone delicious across the bar. In short, love might be the Highway to Heaven, but you'll need more than a hard shoulder to cry on.

Just think of *The Dating Game* as your Highway Code.

We all know we want someone to curl up and watch *Friends* with, someone to love us even when we're grouchy, someone to have mad passionate sex with, someone to make slow, delicious love to, someone who knows that special spot that makes us tingle. Men and women are different (*well done*, Davina!) but we're all looking for love. So love should be simple, right?

Somehow, things aren't quite working out like that. And that's what I'm here to fix.

Just call me Cupid.

IT'S A MAD, MAD WORLD

The way I see it, things are just too complicated. Long gone are the days when Mr Caveman dragged Ms Cavegirl back to his rocky bachelor pad by her hair – not that this is a model we should return to. My hair isn't long enough. But I bet Mr and Miss Caveperson were a lot luckier in love than we are nowadays.

The point is that although – what with sexual equality and liberal licensing laws – dating should be simple, it's not. It's a minefield. And there are a few major reasons why:

♥ **Where are you all?**

I hate to point out the obvious, but if you're going to have a great relationship with someone – even if you're going to have a bad relationship with someone – you have to meet them first. And nobody ever meets anyone new!

OK, so some of us meet loads of people at college – more people than you could seriously need to meet in a lifetime – but university's about being young, free and single. It's about great nights out with your friends and 'Omigod, did I do that?' conversations the next morning. It's a chance to make millions of mistakes in the knowledge that everyone else is so busy cocking up that they won't have time to laugh at you. Of course some people manage to get into a deep and meaningful relationship at university and graduate full of plans for glorious careers, white weddings and picket fences, but generally speaking it all disintegrates the minute you hit the real world. The minute reality hits you.

And the problem with the real world is that opportunities to meet the mate of your dreams don't exactly throw themselves at you, so where are you going to find Mr or Ms Happily-Ever-After?

♥ There's work – you can't help meeting people there – but you've got to be either very brave or very foolish to look on the office as a romantic hunting-ground.

♥ There's meeting your friends' friends, but chances are you've already sized them up and rejected them.

♥ There's your own friends, but you've probably already been there.

♥ There's picking people up in bars, but there's always that little niggling worry that you might end up with an axe-murderer.

The list goes on . . .

So what do you do? You stay single.

♥ **Perfect Girlfriend Syndrome**
Some men are destined for the rocky road to romance because they suffer from Perfect Girlfriend Syndrome. Somewhere in the past, probably when they were young and impressionable, they went out with a Perfect Girl. They probably didn't realise she was Perfect to begin with, but by the time things went horribly wrong, their every impression of what a woman should look, sound, dress and smell like had been formed.

Perfect Girlfriend Syndrome creates a Perfect Nightmare for every woman who follows until the guy realises that the past is past. And unfortunately the fantasy can only be shattered by a reunion with Perfect Girlfriend, when the sufferer can see her for what she really is (which might still be very nice) rather than what he imagines her to be (so nice it hurts). Naturally this course of action is slightly risky and can backfire if she's still Perfect, but there's no other cure.

Women can suffer from this problem too. It's called 'He's no George Clooney'.

♥ **Thirty-Love**
Dating has turned into a spectator sport. We love it! Why do you think *Bridget Jones's Diary* was a bestseller? Why do

you think millions tune in every week to *Friends, Blind Date* and *Ally McBeal*? Why do you think you bought this book? We're all obsessed with love. And never more so than when it's our friends providing the sideshow.

So you get together with someone you like, start making those scary, tentative relationship-noises, look over your shoulder and what do you see? Twenty of your best mates going: *you shouldn't have said that . . . isn't her laugh a bit odd? . . . I liked the last one better . . . I'm not sure about his shoes.*

And you wonder why you get stagefright!

♥ **Anyone for tennis?**
So what happens is that we're all stuck playing games. And unfortunately I don't mean the ones which involve whipped cream, Häagen-Dazs and naked bodies. There are all these stupid rules like:

♥ Never let them know you're keen

♥ Never be the first to say 'I love you'

♥ Don't make yourself too available

If you're not supposed to seem keen, you're not allowed to be honest and you have to keep pretending to be busy, how are you supposed to get past a first date?

It's all so complicated that there's no time to have fun, and call me old-fashioned but I thought we were supposed to *enjoy* dating!

By now you're probably feeling quite relaxed, settling back

and reassuring yourself that you're not to blame for the misery of the modern dating scene. All you have to do is sit there, and it will all come right in the end.

THINK AGAIN!

You've got some serious homework to do before the relationships mess gets untangled. Both men and women have some weird and not-so-wonderful traits, and it's time we sorted them out.

WEIRD WOMEN

What is it with us? We're supposed to be the sensible ones, the ones who actually *want* to make a relationship work, the sensitive ones from Venus who want to talk things through and work things out, but somewhere along the line we've got it **All Screwed Up**. We're scaring men off, the poor loves, and I don't blame them.

♥ **The Big Day**
   How did girls get so obsessed with white frocks, confetti and catching bouquets? I thought we were independent people with minds of our own. So why do I know so many girls – of all ages – who are just gagging for that gold band on their fourth finger? Now I'm not knocking marriage per se (having had one of my own), but this determination to Get A Husband has got to stop. Bridget Jones? Ally McBeal? Whinging singletons? Fools. And there's two big reasons why:

   ♥ Once you start fixating on The Big Day, you become

mysteriously less picky about The Husband. Some of the most fantastic, otherwise sorted women in the world end up living in marital hell, just for the sake of becoming a Mrs.

♥ Men can smell husband-hunters. Once you get in a marrying mindset, you give off desperation vibes, and that's like wearing man-repellent. It's just asking for trouble.

♥ Girl Power

The Spice Girls might not have done much for politics, but they did create Girl Power. And Girl Power's a great idea in principle, but it's turned into an excuse to drink a lot, be rowdy and throw up – in short, to emulate men at their worst. Now I'm sorry girls, but how does turning into crass beer-monsters assert our strength and individuality? It doesn't.

When I was growing up I was part of a gang called the Unsteady Crew – well, it was the eighties and all the gangs had silly names like that then. I was the youngest member, and the only woman, so I made it my mission to be the toughest of them all. I'd out-drink, out-smoke, out-swear, and out-party the lot of them. Now I'll admit I had a great time – most of the time – but being one of the lads wasn't actually as much fun as I'd thought it would be. Men liked me, but they didn't fancy me. It didn't do a lot for my sex life. So, while I'm an independent woman with a life and mind of my own, I'd defend my right to wear skirts and Get Flirty to the death.

What really gets me is that this seems to be a peculiarly British thing. I mean think about it:

♥ French girls are raised to be the epitome of ladylike sophistication. They drink Kir.

♥ Italian girls behave as though they were stuck in the 50s, that smoulderingly sexy *La Dolce Vita* approach.

♥ Spanish girls have the enviable ability to drape themselves elegantly and seductively around almost any piece of furniture.

♥ And English girls? Well, we can down pints, play rugby and sing drinking songs. Very sexy!

And think of the poor guys who have to deal with Girl Power! While the Grrrls are out there yelling drinking songs and puking in the gutters, what are they supposed to do? Tie on a little apron and make us a nice cup of tea? I'm not sure about you, but I'd rather kill myself than date a guy in a frilly apron.

♥ Girly Chats

I love girly chats. There's nothing better (well, almost nothing better . . .) than a good gossip with the girls. You can tell them everything and you know they'll understand. They won't judge you. They'll always listen. They love you pretty much unconditionally. So where's the problem?

The problem is that gaggles of girls terrify men. Think shoals of piranhas, ready and waiting to massacre their dangly bits. They know we tell each other everything, they know we've got a bizarre sense of humour they'll never crack, and it scares the shit out of them to watch us in action. So the thing is to be a bit gentle with them.

♥ Don't jump out of bed after your first shag and spend hours giggling on the phone

♥ Don't go into a huddle with your girly friends and then fall silent when the love of your life arrives

♥ Don't tell him that Serena's new boyfriend has a bendy willy – he doesn't need to know and he'll just wonder what on earth you've said about his

And guys – don't start feeling smug! You and your mates are just as bad.

MYSTERIOUS MEN

♥ Group Sex

Let me make one thing clear: **Sex is not a team sport.** Neither is love, and relationships are definitely a bicycle made for two. So why do men seem to feel they have to play the dating game *together*? We all know men hunt in packs and that's fine – so do women – but you don't necessarily all have to run in the same direction at once.

So why is it that when you see a group of guys, they're either **all** single or **all** coupled-up? It's like some sort of strange domino effect: they're all happily out on the pull together until the leader (Top Cat) gets a serious girlfriend – by which I mean he doesn't share every detail of their sex life with his mates – and then you can just sit back and watch the rest topple headlong into coupledom. Then a few years later Top Cat will get married, and the rest will succumb within two years. At the most. And this can have disastrous effects:

My friend Adam is a gorgeous bloke. He's funny, attractive, thoughtful and intelligent. He'd be a great catch for any girl, but there's one problem: his friends. Ever since school he's been hanging around with this gang who are all perfectly nice, but all perfectly single. They spend their lives running around bars, clubs and pubs, desperately pulling as if it's going out of fashion. They share every gory detail, and 'girlfriend' is a dirty word. But Adam's a bit different, and a while ago he started dating Emily, a fab girl he met in a bar. She made him utterly happy, but when he was with his mates they took the piss so much that in the end he couldn't hack it. He succumbed to the peer pressure and snogged some random girl in the local pub. Unfortunately, she was with Emily's best friend, and I don't think I need to tell you how the story ends. Of course he should have told his mates where to get off, but years of friendship are very difficult to untangle. Tragic.

Now I just know that every girl reading this is sitting there nodding sagely, reminiscing about her Adam. We've all been there: wonderful, caring men who turned into uncontrollable, testosterone-driven animals around their friends. So grow up, guys. Assert your independence!

♥ **Checklist mentality**

I know men are supposed to like things orderly and regimented, but surely military precision shouldn't extend to romance! It seems to me that while women have a biological bodyclock, men have a checklist which goes something like this:

♥ Leave school/college/university

♥ Get job

♥ Get serious girlfriend (marriage material)

♥ Get promoted

♥ Get engaged

♥ Buy house/flat

♥ Get married

Not a lot of room for spontaneity there!

♥ Alpha Males

The thing is, men like to be in control. Genetically, I mean – they can't help it. And while I'm not suggesting that we girls return to the kitchen, Girl Power has made things a bit tricky for guys. That old caveman instinct is telling them to provide for us and protect us, but we don't really seem to need protecting. And we sure as hell aren't starving to death without them. They're not really sure where they stand any more, so cut them a bit of slack, girls. Don't cut their balls off and then expect a good rogering.

♥ The Competitive Streak

While sex isn't a team sport, neither is it a competition. I hate to be the one to break it to you, but we women aren't terribly keen on the whole notch-on-the-bedpost thing. And although you might get to fourth base before she finds out what game you're playing, she sure as hell won't let you into the arena again. So if you're after more than one night of passion, don't take your mates to bed with you – metaphorically speaking. (And I'd recommend waiting until you know the lucky lady quite well before you start trying *literally* to take your mates to bed with you.)

So there you have it. The dilemma. It's a nightmare, isn't it! Forget men being from Mars and women from Venus, we're scarcely in the same solar system. But luckily help is at hand, so just turn the page for my step-by-step guide to dating success!

Of all the Gin Joints in all the Towns in all the World, She walks into Mine

OR

How to Meet a Mate

RELAX – JUST DO IT

Why is that no matter how hard you look for a partner when you're single, none – NONE! – fall at your feet. Forget falling at your feet – they don't even give you the time of day. Your world is suddenly a dateless, mateless, coupled-up hell. While all your friends are planning dirty weekends, you're feeling progressively more green and furry. Even the pizza boy looks a distinct possibility. Something's not right.

Yet, the second you're taken, the opportunities just hurl themselves at you! **Why? Why? Why?** I can't stand it!

My experience of man-hunting has led me to two conclusions (after a lot of research, you understand):

♥ as soon as you start looking, that's when it gets difficult

♥ as soon as you stop looking, it's all roses

Of course, if you're out there determined to search for a mate, chances are you'll end up falling for money or a pretty face – neither of which are, in themselves, bad things. On a cold lonely night they can certainly seem very good things indeed.

However, they are not great foundations on which to build a relationship – money won't buy you love and good looks don't last.

Sod's law dictates that you will meet your perfect mate at the last possible place and time you'd ever expect, and when you are least ready for it: bad hair day, make-up-free and in the old tracky-bums you wear to clean the bathroom. But if you can find a guy or girl who thinks you're irresistible even in your slobby Sunday kit, then you're onto a winner. That's when you've found a relationship to aspire to: a meeting of minds, not solely of the sweaty bits I'd rather not talk about right now.

SO JUST SIT BACK, RELAX AND ENJOY.
LET CUPID DO THE WORK.

If you were going to follow my advice to the letter, this would be a very short chapter with one basic message:

Don't look.

But of course you will look. Everybody looks. Unfortunately they usually look in the wrong direction, but look they do. So, knowing the countless hours you will spend considering outfits, applying make-up (especially, but not only, the girls), tousling hair and then drinking enough to calm your nerves (but hopefully not enough to numb them entirely), here are a number of tips that might prod you along the petal-strewn pathway of love rather than tip you into the musty shed of despair.

TWO KEY POINTS, BEFORE WE PROGRESS ANY FURTHER:

1. **Desperate ain't sexy**
   Look as undesperate as possible. I have no idea what this entails, however I do know that desperate vibes are one of those things people can never see in themselves but can always spot a mile off in others. The desperate give off desperate pheromones, and it's a desperate situation. Why hasn't some scientist studied this yet, invented some anti-desperation roll-on?

   Ask a friend – do I seem desperate? If the answer is no, then go out and swing your pants. If the answer is yes, stay at home and practise nonchalance until you can disguise your despair.

2. **Astrology is a no-no**
   (This only applies to women, because men very sensibly don't give a toss about astrology.)

   Never *ever* ask someone you've just met what their star-sign is. It is the kiss of death. Men hate women who witter on about astrology – partly because the minute they hear the word 'star-sign' they know you're envisaging diamond rings, church bells and white taffeta, and partly because astrology is a load of old tosh anyway.

   But if you're really interested, Geminis are tricky, don't cross Scorpios, and remember that Sagittarius equals good. And Capricorn equals very bad indeed. Unless he's an Adonis Capricorn. Which, as all women know, is a special exception.

DRESSED TO KILL

We'll come back to dressing for a date later, but for now there are a few points to be made about Dressing To Pull. Sorry, that should be Dressing To Kill. Slip of the tongue.

Generally speaking . . .

- ♥ Try to look happy – those desperation vibes come from within, so batten them down with a twinkle in the eye and a big spinach-free smile.

- ♥ Think about the signals you want to send out. Loud, ugly clothes tend, for instance, to say 'Don't come near me'. Or 'I got dressed in the dark'. It's not ideal.

- ♥ Remember that cleanliness is next to Godliness. *Think* dirty by all means. But don't *be* dirty. Don't expect to even get into conversation with the partner of your dreams without clean nails and fresh breath.

- ♥ Dress is a complicated matter. Skinhead haircuts and piercings say a lot, for instance, but it's not always a good message. Remember that men and women who are similarly dressed will be drawn to one another – by which I don't mean that a women in a floral dress will be drawn to a man in a floral dress, but rather that someone super-cool will be drawn to someone else who is super-cool. So watch what you wear!

For Him

- ♥ There are a few items of men's clothing that I simply can't stand. And I suspect I'm not alone. Starting with the last

thing a girl gets to see, ITSY BITSY TEENY WEENY THONGS –
as worn by Euroman and the particular speciality of German tourists, especially the overweight ones who stand
around with their hands on their hips looking terrifyingly
– and hideously – naked. Men – don't go there. Because
women won't want to go there. Thongs are especially
bad – and brace yourself, this might be more detail
than you require – when the man in question has that
fuzzy pubic hair running down the top of his thighs. Nasty.

♥ Also off my personal list are NUT-HUGGERS, those
trousers worn pulled up really high and done up very
tightly with an over-long belt, usually topped off with a
tucked-in T-shirt. WHITE TOWELLING SOCKS are also
OUT OUT OUT, unless worn with trainers and then
preferably during some sporting activity, and clean,
unscuffed, nice SHOES are essential. My grandmother
always said you can judge a man by his shoes. And a
man with scuffed shoes is a man with a scuffed
personality. Buy some polish or shove off.

♥ HAIR is a very important issue: faces should either be
cleanshaven or have at least four days' growth, so that it
is soft. Anything in between hurts – both her face and
your chances. No woman likes snogging a Brillo pad.
Body-hair should simply be there. It doesn't matter if it's
there in copious amounts, but no chest – I repeat, NO
CHEST – should be waxed. Only Mr Universe and
Olympic swimmers are allowed to wax their chests. And
frankly, you don't get many of them to the pound.

♥ HEAD HAIR is another ball-game altogether. Hair should
be worn shortish, youngish, not remotely resembling

70s man (think Terry Wogan and Tony Blackburn – sorry chaps), and not over-gelled. Women like to be able to run their hands through their man's hair without breaking their fingers. Hair should move in the wind – and I don't mean a hurricane.

♥ In short, men should look as if they have paid some attention to their appearance, but not too much attention. Men who look as if they have fussy beauty regimes are not to be trusted. The only excuse a man has to spend more time in the bathroom than a woman is a bowel problem.

For Her

♥ Women's dress for the dating game has to tread that very thin line – thinner than the arse department of a German tourist's thong – between sexy and tarty. Page Three girl shoes with a platform sole and a spike heel may get you attention, but not necessarily the right kind of attention. It might be the kind that offers you £20 for a quickie. Bear in mind what sort of signal you want to give out: sex-kitten-chic but not brassy, or outdoor-girl-homely, but not sexless.

♥ Either way, MAKE-UP should be scarce – you might have worn your war-paint two inches thick when you were thirteen, but you're a grown-up now and shouldn't look like you've been experimenting at your mum's dressing-table. A little goes a long way. A woman in thick make-up is like a man with a bushy beard – they've both got something to hide.

♥ Whatever you're wearing should be APPROPRIATE – wearing a wetsuit to a bar, for instance, while innovative

22

and original, is not necessarily advisable. Do a little research beforehand, and dress accordingly. I once went to a big TV company's Christmas party, having been told that they were wild, raucous affairs where everybody made a real effort. When I turned up, everyone was dressed in casual workwear. I, on the other hand, wore a sexy Santa outfit with hat, heels and fur-trimmed red mini. Ho, ho, ho.

So now you're all dressed up, and looking for somewhere to go. It's strange but true that most men are under the impression that they don't ever meet women. Women always meet them. Ask a man where he'd go to meet a woman and, after a bemused five-minute blank, he'll say 'at a sports event'. Now, in fantasyland he might be able to combine finding romance with supporting his local team, but women reading this will know that's highly unlikely. I don't know a single girl so desperate to meet men that she'll hang around outside a football ground. Well, not that many.

The point is that you really ought to think very hard about where you go hunting for the prospective love of your life, but as my guess is that most of you will simply take a trip to the nearest bar, we'll start there.

BAR FLIES

Meeting people in clubs, pubs and bars is sadly much harder than everyone thinks – it's not just a question of swanning in, ordering a dry Martini, perching elegantly on a barstool and waiting for the eligible suitors to arrive. When the bar closes you'll be single, drunk and depressed instead of just single, as anybody who's ever tried it and ended up weeping into their drink will know.

Location! Location! Location!

It stands to reason that if you want to meet a particular type, you need to socialise where that type tends to congregate. This might smack of desperation, but all's fair in love and war. Especially love.

Take Jenny. At the moment she's into City boys. She's convinced herself that she's ready to marry for money (Gold-digger! Who said that?) and reckons city boys must pull in a good salary. They certainly talk about money enough of the time. So, although she lives about an hour away from the City, that's where she goes out. She's done her homework, hits the right pubs and bars and finds herself surrounded by men with stripy shirts, loose ties, wide-boy accents and a remarkable talent for boasting about how big it is. Their wallet, that is. She's made.

By the same token, she's somehow managed to wangle a ticket to the executive box of her local premier division football team. Does she like football? Not a bit of it. She thinks Vialli is a wine. But does she go? You betcha. For there, not only does she find many a wealthy man, but she is often virtually the only girl, so she gets loads of attention (which of course has nothing to do with the belt-cum-skirt she's wearing). It beats being down on the terraces, she says, all those grubby types disappearing right after the game to go and buy their death-burgers. Better class of chat-up entirely.

But back in the real world, a good place to go is somewhere you see people who look like you. If you think you're a bit cool, go to trendy bars full of other people who think they're a bit cool. A Goth is unlikely to meet another Goth at a super-swanky members-only bar. A sports fan is unlikely to find someone who shares their passion at a poetry reading.

Safety in numbers

Women tend to travel in packs, believing that a big group with an in-built support system, confidence-booster and rejection-soother is The Way Forward. Unfortunately, this is an absolute lie. As any man will tell you, a group of more than three women is an absolutely terrifying experience and certainly not conducive to romance. Few men have the brass balls to approach a large, swaying, braying gaggle of girls. The brave man who does deserves *muchos respect* but he is a rare beast indeed. Large gaggles of girls have killed most of them off.

So although safety in numbers is a good thing, don't go out with a huge group of friends if you're looking for love. This makes you seem utterly unapproachable to anyone less fearless than Attila the Hun. And even Attila hated bars, especially crowded ones. Try going out with just a few friends on the mutual understanding that if one of you takes off with some sexy stranger, nobody will be offended. After all, you can see your mates anytime. And hot dating opportunities don't come along every day.

Going solo

As for your other option, hanging around alone in bars, what you need is the right attitude. Male or female, you have to look available – but not as if you expect to be paid for your time. If you're not careful, you'll get to know the barman's life story – the hilarious details of his brother's stag night, how Port Talbot United are doing this season – and the flock of bright, witty, gorgeous, single people eyeing you up will just assume you're waiting for somebody.

If you're on your own and on the pull, the important thing is to look like you're interested – but interested in the right things. The decor is fine. The dancing is fine. Both give you the opportunity to look around and size up the possible pickings. But seeming riveted by your drink simply makes you look lonely.

The key is, then, to remember that the eyes have it. There's a simple formula:

♥ Eye contact 1

♥ Eye contact 2

♥ Smile

♥ A simple (and admittedly very brave) offer to buy your would-be love interest a drink. No chat-up lines, just polite, simple, unthreatening conversation – this is not the time to use the 'Your eyes are like spanners – every time I look into them my nuts tighten' line.

Going in for the kill

If you're a man, and the girl you're after is with a bunch of mates, follow steps 1-3 above and then try to detach the object of your affection from the group. Think sheepdog trials and you won't go far wrong. A good trick is beckoning her over, but girls should note that this does not work with men who will, when one of their group is beckoned, collectively start hollering 'Get in there, my son!' Not a pretty sight.

But this isn't to say that girls are off the hook. The girl's role is to be very clear with her signals. The odd glance, a cursory raised eyebrow is simply not enough because men are completely rubbish at reading come-on signals. So make your body semaphore easy-to-read.

One useful trick is that if your prospective beloved's eyes dilate when you first speak, it means they fancy you. Eyes also dilate when someone takes cocaine, but at least you'll know they're either interested or a crack-head. It narrows the options. Speaking of drugs, decide whether you're after a smoker or non-smoker depending on your taste. Taste being the operative word: the old 'kissing an ashtray' cliché is well-worn for a reason. Smokers look unhealthy, their clothes smell, their homes are always grey and they will die young. Healthy, clean-smelling people with a decent life expectancy are my preference – but as I said, it's a personal one.

D'you come here often?

All of which brings us on to chat-up lines, and I have just one thing to say here: CHAT-UP LINES DO NOT WORK. You just sound like a cheap pick-up merchant. I have only ever heard two chat-up lines that have made any impression on me. One entailed being asked to guess a number from one to ten.

'Seven,' I said.

'Wrong,' he replied. 'Take your clothes off.'

Well, it appealed to me. The other is too dirty to print.

Chat-up lines just can't be relied on. Most of them make the person saying them look a bit of an idiot. Even when you hear one that somebody absolutely swears by, claims several successful evenings and a number of new friends by, it's still hard to believe.

Take Paul. His favourite line – and he says it works nearly every time – is painful to listen to. But he says that if he's with a group of guys out at a club or in a pub and they want to get mingling with a group of girls there, one of them goes up to the group and, after they've given him all the usual 'what do you want?' stuff and the conversation has gone silent – says:

"Well, all we need now is a ten-foot penguin."

"A what?" they all reply in unison.

"A ten-foot penguin," he'll repeat, entirely straight-faced.

"What do we need a ten-foot penguin for?" they ask, by this time no doubt sensing a terrible punch-line. And he says:

"Something to break the ice with."

Paul's mates are, thankfully, sanguine about the outcome. If the girls fall about laughing – which Paul swears nearly always happens – then they're all in for a good night together. If there's a dead calm and blank faces, then they're not the kind of girls they're interested in anyway. So I guess they win either way.

But, despite (or maybe because of) this supposed success story, I'm sticking to my guns. Chat-up lines are a bad idea.

Chatting up is in fact much easier for girls. While a man has to rely on a dazzling smile, pert buttocks and the kind-heartedness (or sheer desperation) of the object of his probably sozzled affection, women have it made. They can talk gibberish and have a man spellbound because he is so rarely asked anything other than the time by a woman that he will be instantly enraptured by practically any female who will briefly make him the centre of her attention. She can be abstract ('Did you know that the Forth Bridge weighs six million tons?'), tedious ('The music here is great') or even direct ('You've got lovely lips'). It doesn't matter. Simply to have been approached is enough to have any single man – and, sad to say, quite a few unsingle men – fawning at the brave girl's feet. It shocks them into submission.

My friend Tania is great at approaching men – she's one of the bravest girls I know. I'd definitely never have the nerve to pull off some of her pulls. She's just brimming with confidence, so she strides up to the man she's after, looks him in the eyes, introduces herself and they're off! I've never seen it fail. Her most notorious pull, however, was Max, where there wasn't actually any chatting involved at all. There they both were, two strangers in a nightclub, spending half the evening drinking – which always helps lower the inhibitions – and the other half eyeing each other up. Finally he gesticulated that he was leaving and suggested – all through nods and winks, mind – that she should follow him. So two minutes later out she went. And there he was, waiting in the car park. And do you know what his first reaction was? "I can't believe you followed me out!" He was really shocked that she went for it, as well as totally impressed by her balls (if you see what I mean). His second reaction was to get her into a passionate clinch, and they ended up going out with each other for fifteen months. Astonishing, but true.

Getting an eye-full

One small point to put men's minds at rest. You might think girls try to catch a glimpse of your trouser bulges during conversation, but it simply isn't true. Girls don't do this – not because we're not instinctively drawn to your trouser region, but because after countless disappointments and surprises we've learned that there is nothing to be gained from trying to get a sneak preview. Unless the guy is wearing skin-tight Lycra – and let's face it, if he's wearing skin-tight Lycra in a bar then he is a definite no-no – there really isn't much to look at. Besides, the bulge is no indication of its potential. Nor are the size of his feet – though I think there might be some parallel with the size of his hands. That's my observation: big hands, monster gloves.

Conversely, it is absolutely true that men have a nasty habit of addressing all their remarks to a woman's breasts. Women, especially those with an ample bosom, get this all the time and it drives them spare. Any man who can hold eye-contact – even if he has to mentally recite the names of the 1966 England world-cup squad to keep himself distracted – will be heartily rewarded at a later date. It will be a rare, worthwhile and greatly appreciated effort.

And remember that – whatever Girl Power and political correctness dictate – a woman loves a gentleman. Especially if he has previously tried to come across as a bit of a bloke. Chivalrous, gentlemanly behaviour – think Sean Connery – is a sign that he has a heart as well as the ability to drink loads of beer. This is a good sign.

Similarly, a man loves a lady. Don't for God's sake be girly, but be feminine. Think Lauren Bacall and you won't go wrong.

THE BLIND DATE

Love might be blind, but blind dates are stupid. Say it with me:

BLIND DATES ARE A BAD IDEA.

They rarely make it to the dessert menu, let alone a second meeting.

I've been on one blind date, and I had a perfectly pleasant evening with a perfectly nice man, but I knew from the second I laid eyes on him that that was all I was ever going to lie on him.

The fact is that most people get talking because there's some kind of physical attraction. Let's be realistic: you go out on a date with someone because they've got a bum you want to squeeze. However slight, the biological connection is what brings us together. On a blind date, however, you're stuck with a wildly inaccurate description from a biased friend – let's face it, you'd never agree to go on a blind date with someone described as dull and portly but a very good golfer.

A couple of years ago, my friend Tony was going through such a dry spell that he succumbed to his best mate's attempts to set him up with this girl, Gabriella. They'd be perfect for each other, his best mate assured him. Soul mates, in fact. Tony got to the restaurant and was then forced to sit through a three-hour dinner with a girl whose idea of a good laugh was to grab the waiter's crotch to get his attention. A girl whose idea of a good laugh was to speculate loudly about the sex

> lives of the surrounding diners. A girl with a laugh which would have embarrassed a hyena. Tony didn't see Gabriella again. In fact he didn't see his best mate again either.

Even in the best of circumstances, blind dates are stressful: you're always having to perform, always having to pretend that you actually *like* the other person. Remember: the show ain't over 'til the fat lady brings the bill. And that can be an awfully long time.

WHEREFORE ART THOU? – THE SET-UP

Going out to find the stranger of your dreams in a crowded bar might be hard, but it's infinitely more reliable than being fixed up by a friend. I don't know why friends get it so wrong, but they do. Over and over again.

> I had two single friends who I was absolutely convinced would be ideal for each other. I invited both over for dinner – as part of a big group, without telling either of them about my matchmaking plans – but they just didn't hit it off. They were both lovely, intelligent people but it just didn't happen. So I got them together again. Still nothing. But I wouldn't let it lie. Again I contrived a situation in which they'd meet, and eventually they started to twig. In the end, they both sat down and told me to please give it up – they liked each other, but that was it. And that was all there was ever going to be. You see even the professional gets it wrong sometimes.

Pushy friends can definitely lose their appeal – and I speak as a pushy friend. If I have a group of single friends over for dinner, and I think someone isn't selling themselves sufficiently – despite the fact that they're perfectly savvy adults – I have to bite my tongue to stop myself diving in with: "By the way, everyone, Julie's really quite wonderful, a fantastic cook, top of her field and has an amazing body when she takes her clothes off". It would put everyone off their asparagus tips.

Matchmaker friends are often more keen for you to be hooked-up than you are. It's probably more convenient for them. This zealousness tends to make for a situation in which Mr or Ms Average is made to sound almost inhumanly perfect. And disappointment is bound to follow.

But surely friends must get it right once in a while, and there are advantages to meeting someone this way. For one thing, you should hopefully get a pretty definite promise that they're not a mad axe-murderer. For another, you can have an honest assessment of your new beau from someone you trust – or at least someone whose foibles you're aware of. Your friend will be able to tell you what they're really like, what they're into, what they're looking for in life – and love.

BUT be wary of any friend who knows too much – the way she brushes her teeth, which side of the bed he prefers, that she has a penchant for curry-flavoured condoms, that kind of thing. Chances are, this friend has an ulterior motive.

DATING AGENCIES

Dating agencies. I know what you're thinking:

> • Sad, balding, middle-aged accountant
> seeks mousy librarian for early-evening
> scrabble and life of inertia.

But you might be surprised.

OK a dating agency *might* be a disaster, but in my book (and this is, after all, my book) it's likely to be a much less nerve-wracking disaster than a blind date. Or screwing up the courage to chat someone up in a bar. At least the other person actually wants to meet you – even if you then hate each other on sight. Joining an agency might be an act of complete madness, but take it with a big pinch of salt and at least you'll have a laugh. Embrace the absurdity of it all!

And if you're still feeling queasy at the idea of bringing in the professionals, look at it this way: you'd hire a nanny to look after your children or a cleaner to tidy your house, wouldn't you? A dating agency is simply another utility. Much as you take a car to a mechanic, a PC to an IT expert, an ache to the doctor, you take your floundering love-life to a dating agency.

Of course once you've chosen your agency – and personally I'd go for quite a well-known one with one of the less cheesy names; don't look for a dating agency in a phone box, and steer clear of anything with the words 'naughty' or 'sensual' in the title – then you're on to filling out likes and dislikes forms, providing passport-sized photographs (in which, by the way, it's been scientifically-proven impossible to look even remotely attractive) and assessing whether you like the look of someone else with half their head missing because the stool was too high. It might seem unromantic but, let's be honest, this is exactly the same calculated process you go through when you meet someone anyway. So you might as well be accurate and get it all down on paper. Think of it as precision dating.

The secret is to involve your friends to take the edge of what might feel like a lonely – and somewhat bizarre – business. Ask them what they think of the men or women you've got to choose from. If you make it to a second date, start introducing your new sweetheart to your friends. In short, once an introduction has been made, ignore the fact that your match-maker can perform 38,000 operations per second and has a 600 megabyte memory, and carry on as though you'd met in a more normal way – as if friends and not an IBM had introduced you. You may well meet lots of people before you hit paydirt, but you'll have a hell of a time along the way.

A friend of mine, Lucy, works for a dating agency and tells me that they've honestly got quite a high success rate. She repeatedly informs me that their clients are definitely PLU (People Like Us – she's a bit of a sloane), and 'really very nice professional people'. And she assures me that she and her co-workers don't laugh at them behind their back. Well, not all of them. There is one guy there, however, who seems destined to be on their books for ever: twenty-nine-year-old Gary is about five foot three, with a Kevin Keegan haircut (the 70s version) and a penchant for loud shirts with even louder ties. He's looking for a mid-thirties professional woman (preferably a lawyer or a banker) to share his interest in fantasy games (and we're talking Dungeons & Dragons, not whips and leather). He wants to find someone to play with his magic sword. Lucy's single herself at the moment, but doesn't seem terribly keen to join a dating agency. I'm not sure why . . .

THE SMALL ADS

My stance on small ads is much the same as my stance on blind dates:

DATING THROUGH THE SMALL ADS IS A BAD IDEA

You've got all the potential embarrassment of a dating agency, without the not-inconsiderable benefit of a photograph and a middle man to root out the dodgy types.

But if you really must reply to a small ad, think carefully about where you plan to meet. If your date suggests you meet at dusk in the park, this is **not** someone you want to get to know. If you can't arrange to meet in a group, meet in broad daylight and in a public place. This isn't the voice of doom speaking, but these can be dark times and Mr Romance should always live on the other side of town from Mr Creepy.

Of course, you also have to remember that the small-ad is the very heart of the classic oversell. In the small ads, every man is George Clooney, every woman is

Jennifer Lopez. Nobody is fat. Nobody is neurotic. It's Oz. It's Disneyland. It's not to be trusted.

Of course, being dishonest in your personal description is self-defeating and always disappointing – when George and Jennifer meet and its more like George and Mildred, they deserve each other – but neither should you be *too* honest. Admitting to halitosis or veruccas is not only providing rather more detail than anybody requires at this stage, but will also win you *nul points* in the dating game. And it's better to aim to touch the heart than the nether regions. 'Big tanned hunk of a fireman, with trust-fund and new novel out in hardback' really isn't as effective as 'normal-looking guy needs looking after'. Of course if you really are a big tanned hunk of a fireman etc. then don't hold back, but why are you using the small ads? Oops. Didn't mean to say that. Just joking.

The skill is to read between the lines. Try your hand at a bit of psychological interpretation. Is, perhaps, a small ad placed in *The Times* suggestive of a classier type of person than someone who announces that they're looking for love in the free ads section of a local paper between the second-hand washing machines and clapped-out cars? And surely a GSOH should shine through in the ad itself, rather than having to be spelt out (or not). Just make sure you retain your GSOI – Good Sense Of Irony.

BEYOND THE SMALL ADS . . .

While the Cupid small ads require a sense of adventure, other points of contact generally require a sense of suicide. Telephone chat lines are creepy in the extreme, generally revolting and should not lead to any meeting of any description. They are run by women in their sixties who, despite what they say, look about as much like Jo Guest as Anne Widdecombe looks like Raquel Welsh, and who are not wearing a pink lacy transparent camisole, crotchless French knickers and suspenders, but an old sweatshirt, grey baggy-arsed jogging bottoms and fluffy slippers. They bring seedy men to orgasm while filing their nails. This is NOT romantic. Besides, they cost at least 50p a minute and show up on your itemised bill. Leave well alone.

Better than all these options is my friend Lisa's idea. She and nine other single friends get together once a month to form a kind of committee. They choose a venue and each brings along ten single friends to a big singles party. Before the party they pair off people they think would get along, who meet for an hour or so beforehand. If they hit it off, great. If not, they don't have to spend a painful evening together or break it off awkwardly. They just go on to the party where they meet lots of other single people. It's a great idea. I might nick it and try and make a bit of money.

THE BEST 'FRIEND'

There are two schools of thought when it comes to becoming more than just good friends with a good friend.

- ♥ The first says that it's A GREAT IDEA: you already know each other very well, you know each other ticks and foibles, you can't be surprised by a bad side, it would be a safe and dependable start to a relationship.

- ♥ The second says that it's A VERY BAD IDEA: you already know each other very well, you know each other ticks and foibles, you can't be surprised by a bad side, it would be a safe and dependable start to a relationship.

It depends what you're after. If friendship is the essential foundation of any long-lasting relationship (which I believe it should be), then it stands to reason that getting together with a friend makes perfect sense.

You can imagine the situation: one of you is tired and upset, emotionally vulnerable, weepy, and the other is solid and there for you. Comforting words turn into a comforting hug, which turns into a comforting peck on the forehead, which turns into a comfortable kiss on the lips, which turns into a comfortable snog, which turns into a long, slow, comfortable scrabble around for your underwear ten minutes later.

Pandora's box has been opened. Especially if her name really is Pandora.

It's easy for one thing to turn into something completely different entirely, but the problem is you have a lot to lose. Can you go back to what you were before? It's almost like the Fall. Having known each other in the Biblical sense, it's hard to return to that innocent time of unspoken understandings and loaded touches. It's impossible to return to blissful ignorance of each others' nooks and crannies.

But staying just best friends with a best friend of the opposite sex isn't easy. As *When Harry Met Sally* taught us, sex always gets in the way. It's birds and bees stuff. If you really love someone, you know they love you, you spend a lot of time together and – as best friends often are – you're very cuddly with each other, it's not altogether surprising that it's easy to end up in bed together. It just happens.

So, in an ideal world, you need to work out – before the sexual chemistry explodes – whether you really want a lifetime of passion together or whether shagging is just a kind of prolonged hug. And the only way to do that is to talk about it first. This sounds like a horrific idea – almost as scary as actually doing the dirty deed – because you've still gone public with it, you've let the proverbial cat out of the bag and now it's going to pee on your mattress and rip up the sofa. And yes, it will be hugely embarrassing. But better out than in.

If you really can't face that, then you could try asking a mutual friend to drop a hint and report back to you on the response – Do they fancy you too? Do they think it would be a good idea? The childishness of this might make you feel like you're back at school. But that's OK. You've probably known each other since then anyway.

I know Best Friends are really tempting, particularly if you're both going through a dry spell, and it can work out fantastically well! But it can also end in disaster. You've been warned!

My friend Victoria used to have a male best friend – Tom. They loved each other to death, had exactly the same sense of humour, and used to embark on the most extraordinary – and hilarious – nights out together. They'd go out to really tacky bars for pulling competitions and the winner was the person who found someone to go home with first. Which was fine – if a bit strange, but who am I to judge? – until one night neither of them pulled. Love obviously wasn't in the air, because the barman called time and they were both still standing there, single. So – in the spirit of the game – they decided to go home together. They pulled each other and announced it was a draw. A few days later they went out again, and – surprise – it was a draw again. It all started to get a bit of a habit, but they never talked about it – after all, it wasn't like they were *dating* or anything. It was just a sex thing. No emotional ties. Just best friends who had sex sometimes. Honest. Then, after about a month, they went out on one of their big nights out and it wasn't a draw. Victoria won, going home with a rather sexy mover called James. And Tom was devastated. Being devastated wasn't playing by the rules, so he didn't say anything – but the next week he won in the first half-hour. Victoria was not pleased. Anyway, I won't go into the gory details of it all, but take it from me that it was horrible. And a very good friendship exploded.

OFFICE ROMANCE

Flirting by the filing cabinets
Snogging in the stationery cupboard
Sex over the boss's desk

What is it about office romances? Sex in the office always seems to come high in lists of favourite sexual fantasies, and it's there in every top ten of 'the most exciting places you've had sex'. Why is this? Is it some kind of revolutionary statement against authority? A thrill from the knowledge that you know something your boss doesn't about his desk? Or is it just naughty?

Either way, office romances can be very exciting. But very hard! So the secret of a sizzlingly sexy office romance (and the secret to not getting fired) is to keep it a secret for as long as possible. Make the most of that 1500-volt sexual spark every time you brush past each other in the corridor, every time you manage to sneak a forbidden touch in a crowded elevator. We all know that the overwhelming, uncontrollable, heady excitement of a new affair eventually wanes, but keeping a secret certainly helps to prolong it.

But of course it won't be a secret for long. Colleagues *always* pick up on those little signs that you always think you're being so discreet about – I mean what do you expect? Most offices are just a bunch of bored or irritated people looking for a bit of juicy gossip to spice up their lives.

A friend of mine had an office romance and thought she was being so careful. But, mysteriously, after a few months it became clear that people had known she was seeing this guy for months. How did we know, she asked? Because she'd let slip that he'd given her a Christmas present – and this present was just a *little* bit too big to be purely friendly. She'd only mentioned the present to one person, but within hours the gossip had spread around the entire building like bad flu.

Some signs are more obvious. When I'm seeing someone I walk around on my toes all the time, with a silly happy look on my face (not to mention the man-rash). Anyone who knows me knows immediately that there's a man involved. So if you're as transparent as me, you'll probably need to invent a new relationship outside of work as no-one will believe you're still single.

The thing to remember is, once you've got past the whole

shagging in the lift thing all manner of problems arise. Once you go public the illicit excitement disappears, and the feeling of guilt and horrendous embarrassment every time someone sees you talking (even if you're discussing unsexy things like flow charts and photocopier toner) sets in. It can be a complete nightmare! And the fact that you'll spend half your working day blushing doesn't make it any easier!

Some companies are even very strict about relationships between employees (surely a red rag to a load of horny bulls?) but the problems are generally more personal than that. Nepotism. Discipline (not the bedroom variety). Ms Sales Manager having to tell Mr Marketing Executive his performance isn't up to standard. And of course there's the other, really tricky issue of how much time you'll end up spending together. You might love your mate truly madly and deeply, but do you really love them twenty-four hours a day? It's a tall order. Work inevitably spills over into personal time, and vice versa, and this won't be popular with the management – even if you are the management.

Then of course there's the hideous problem of still having to work together after you've split up. You end up having to build ineffectual walls of Post-It notes between each other. Refusing to speak to your colleague on the basis that she's too immature to understand you doesn't tend to go down very well. And snapping 'you're just saying that because I wouldn't have anal sex with you' is *not* an appropriate response when your ex-lover disagrees with your brilliant new marketing plan. Especially not if you're in a meeting. It's a complete nightmare.

Of course there *are* pluses to dating someone you work with – you've probably got similar interests for a start – but it's only worth embarking on if it's really going to last.

Otherwise it just gets terribly complicated. Bizarrely enough, I was out the other night with six friends, three of whom are in good relationships with people they work with. Two of them are actually living with their office romance now, and they're all blissfully happy. But surely these three must be the exception to the rule. And they all work in the same office – which possibly says more about their particular office environment than office romances generally. Must be something in the water.

**The moral is: if you're thinking of pulling
at the office, FORGET IT!
You'll thank me.**

None of which is to say that the office party won't be a hot-bed of torrid inter-employee activity, all seemingly forgotten by the next day when the alcoholic haze has settled.

A good friend of mine, Sara, had the best snog of her life at the office Christmas party. Nothing exceptional in that, you might think. But it's usually done with some subtlety – under a desk perhaps, or in a darkened cupboard. Not in the middle of the dance floor with the entire office standing around watching them, jaws dropped. Sometimes there's no time like the present. You can deal with the inevitable flak later. What's going on in your pants *now* is much more important.

Why is it that such mini-flings are considered entirely acceptable, barely worth mentioning and no more than a day's worth of gossip? I don't understand. I would be gossiping about them for weeks and weeks.

VISUALISATION

This is a weird one. And I'm only including it under duress because a friend of mine swears by it. I take no responsibility for it whatsoever.

The theory is this: if you imagine the guy or girl you want to meet hard enough, they will eventually fall into your lap. This takes all the pressure off – you don't have to find suitable bars to hang around, practice your chat-up technique or sit through twelve tortuous dinners set up by a dating agency. All you do is sit around and imagine your perfect partner. And if you think it, he/she will come.

I know, it sounds nuts. But I have to admit that my friend Josie has had a lot of success with it.

About this time last year Josie was very cross indeed because she was experiencing a bit of a dry patch. There she was – twenty-three, gorgeous, witty and smart – and she was stranded in the love desert. So she started fixating on what she wanted – an architect. She decided an architect was a good bet because he would be:

♥   Artistically-minded

♥   Employed

♥   Intelligent

Of course I told her it was a complete waste of time, but she carried on visualising and two months later a friend asked her to a birthday party. She turned up and what did she find? Three architects. Yes, three! She took a good look at them, chose the nicest, and went out on a few dates with him. It didn't work out in the end, but the visualisation had certainly done the trick.

After the architect experience, she decided that she should maybe be a bit less precise – three architects was pushing it. So she concentrated on Artistic, Employed and Intelligent, and a week later ran into an old friend who – it turned out – was now an illustrator. So they dated for a while, and when it went wrong she visualised again and ended up with a lighting designer. They're still together, and blissfully happy.

As I said I'm deeply distrustful of visualisation, and if you're visualising someone whose vision of perfection isn't you you'll be out of luck, but with results like that I just had to share her secret!

TRICKS OF THE TRADE

OK, we've covered all the obvious territory. But if bars, clubs, friends, co-workers and dating agencies aren't doing it for you, here are a few extra tips for those really desperate situations.

For Him

Baby Power

Women are complete suckers for men with babies. Our eyes dilate when we see a baby – it's an unavoidable biological fact. And the big plus is – for the single, girl-hunting male – it doesn't matter whose baby is it. Just holding one will demonstrate your caring, sharing, sensitive side. And you'll find most parents surprisingly willing to lend you one for an hour or two, which is useful.

It does have to be a baby, mind. A toddler with a mind of his or her own is far too demanding for a cruising singleton, but babies! Ahhhh! Remember that black and white poster of the bare-chested, pec-proud Athena man cradling his bundle of joy? Women are still dreaming about that poster.

Flash your cash

Men, in particular, often think that flashing money around will draw women to them. They're right, up to a point and with a certain type of woman – the type who will bleed him dry and then move onto the next sucker. Not a good type to go for. Men believe that wealth and power is to women what long legs and big knockers are to them – an ideal combination. But any old banker can have a flash sportscar.

> I once knew a City guy – I can't quite bring myself to call him a friend – who was utterly convinced that all women were after was money. He was, to say the least, *majorly* unreconstructed. His wooing technique consisted of delivering a bottle of champagne to the lucky lady's table and then, once she'd been

steamrollered into letting him join her, shooting his cuffs a lot to display his Rolex and drumming his fingers on the table to draw attention to his ostentatiously large gold signet ring while talking loudly about his pad in Mayfair, the state of his share portfolio and his new convertible Beamer. He was constantly surprised when women turned down his generous offer of a date. *Oh, puh-leeease!*

Puppy Power

People with dogs – like people at bus stops, or sharing an umbrella (now there's a good idea . . .) – always talk to other people with dogs. It's hard to avoid a chat when your beloved pets are sniffing each other's bottoms.

The great thing about this is that the dog doesn't even have to be yours, so you don't have to worry about going to the park when it's pouring with rain. Weather permitting, you can just pop round to your friend's and borrow the dog when you're feeling particularly in need of love. Just like babies.

Beware of people you see a lot wandering around a park without a dog. They've either missed the point or are up to no good. You want a dog-walker. Not a stalker.

Dance classes

And no, I don't mean waltzing.

Now guys, I know you're sitting there paralysed with horror at the thought of doing something as *girly* as going to a dance class, but **that's the point**. If you're looking for girls, you have to accept that you might have to venture into the territory of things they like. And what we're talking here is salsa, which is **seriously sexy**. All those gyrating hips and thrusting pelvises are guaranteed to get you all in the mood – and course you're allowed to get Up Close And Personal before you've even been properly introduced. No chatting up! The pressure's off! And if you can't find something to say to a girl you've just spent half an hour pressed up against, gyrating madly, then I give up. Get thee to a monastery!

But there's one thing that, as a responsible adult, I feel I should point out. I firmly believe that salsa classes are actually a cult. Once you start going, they've got you. And they won't let you go. You'll be forced to spend every Wednesday evening of the rest of your life downing tequila and strutting your stuff to mad Spanish music. But at least you'll have a good time. And you're bound to pull.

Get hot and sweaty!

A man in some kind of sports kit can be utterly irresistible. It's one of life's great mysteries why women find sporty men so dreamy. Grunting and sweating a lot obviously have certain connotations, but just because a man can score on the pitch doesn't mean he can follow through off it.

Tennis whites look great against a tan, but I'm afraid the sexiest look is a grubby man who looks as if he's just walked off the rugby pitch. This isn't altogether convenient – there's only so far you can get covered in blood and caked in mud before people start avoiding you – so the gym is often a good place to begin a romance: not only do you get to check out each other's lean and well-honed physiques but you get to sweat a lot.

Dressing up

So sporty men can be irresistibly sexy but, to be honest, it's more about the outfit than the sweat. Which is what makes men in uniform – with some notable exceptions – so utterly delicious.

My friend Jenny (yes, her of City boy fame) also has a bit of a thing for men in uniform. She says it's an authority thing – she likes a man who's in control. But it all went horribly wrong a few years ago when we were out in a pub in Salisbury (don't ask why we were in Salisbury) and she noticed a sexy-looking soldier by the bar. Fair enough, we all agreed, there are lots of army types wandering around Salisbury plain, and she sidled over to meet him. He was even sexier up close (although she was most definitely half-cut by this point), and as she batted her eyelids and smiled sexily up at him, all the while managing to maintain a perfect stream of innuendo-laden smalltalk, visions of slowly undoing those shiny buttons ran riot in her brain. Unsurprisingly (if you know Jenny), she returned with him to his flat – although even in her intoxicated state she was surprised he didn't live in barracks or something – and was horrified when, as she reached out to undo the first of the shiny buttons, she discovered that it was a fake. All the buttons were. And underneath them was a decidedly unsexy piece of Velcro. As she looked bemusedly up at him, she saw his face crack into a broad smile. He wasn't a soldier at all. He was a stripper. But the uniform went down so well with the girls who paid him to take it off that he figured it would improve his pulling technique. And he was right.

When I was younger I was mad about motorbikes, and a biker outfit – the leather jacket and helmet – still does it for me. Forget the bike – a man wandering around with a helmet has much the same effect. You could say I'm obsessed.

I'm also a sucker for firemen. Not because I get excited about big yellow helmets, long hoses and reflective strips, but because they put their life on the line for others. It's the old fairytale princess-in-the-tower fantasy – well, that and an instinctive attraction to caring men. Of course there are also lots of juicy Freudian elements to a fireman's job, but it's probably best that we don't explore sliding down poles and rescuing pussies in too much detail. Suffice to say that authority and action are the key ingredients for the guy in uniform – Ronald McDonald is not where it's at . . .

For Her

Shopping (1)

So we women are supposed to be obsessed with shopping – make the most of it! Hanging around the supermarket, squeezing those juicy aubergines and sizing up the courgettes gets you in the mood, and gives you the nerve to approach blokes. But make sure you go for the single ones – if Live-In-Girlfriend is just round the corner selecting a bumper pack of heavy-duty Durex she'll be most miffed to come back and find you chatting up the love of her life. So watch out for lurking females.

Another clue to his single status is in his shopping. If he's buying 'meal for two' packs of everything then keep away – if he hasn't got a girlfriend he's a greedy pig, and you're not interested either way. If he's buying salad, then he's definitely coupled-up. But if he's looking uncertainly at the single steak portions, hesitating over the herbs and spices or piling the ready-made microwaveable curries into his trolley, then **go for it**! Catch his eye over the cold meat counter, ask his advice about spicy sauces, reach for the same tin as him and hope that when your hands meet, you'll both feel that electricity . . .

A couple more handy tips:

♥ Avoid those men who buy nothing but reconstituted junk food – a man who lives on crisps, pop-tarts and Coke is really **not** what you want

♥ If at all possible, choose a man who's buying at least **something** related to cleaning – Jif, Fairy Liquid, jaycloths, Pledge – you don't want a slob

Hot and Sweaty!
The gym approach works for women as well, but there's one key point to remember: women need to learn to sweat to order and in all the right places:

♥ Between the breasts is good.

♥ Under the arms is not so good.

Careful applications of copious amounts of anti-perspirant can help you to achieve this effect. Then just get on that treadmill, have a look around, and start catching eyes in the mirror!

One note of caution: if you're going for the gym pick-up, choose your target with care. Muscled and toned is good, but **too** muscled and toned and you could end up pulling more than just a man.

My friend Sarah decided the gym was the place to find her perfect partner, and chose one in South Kensington very carefully: good area, lots of wealthy professional types, and a slightly higher proportion of men than women. She started going religiously, and soon saw one regular who took her fancy – he was tanned, toned and <u>really</u> big. Just her type. It didn't take much sideways glancing, deep stretching and tactical sweating to get his attention, and they ended up dating. She'd bagged her man. The only problem was that he was a real gym freak. He looked lovely, but he was crazy about working out together. Or maybe just crazy. After a brave – and painful – fortnight of two-hour workouts and early-morning runs, she had to give up. There's fit and there's obsessive, and he'd not only gone way past obsessive but sailed into nut territory.

Shopping (2)

Once you've mastered supermarket shopping (and no, I don't mean for food), it's time to move on to the more specialised versions. It's simple: decide on the kind of man you want to meet, and shop accordingly. You wouldn't go to a fishmonger's to buy perfume, so you just need to apply the same theory to man-shopping.

♥ If you're looking for intelligent, educated and great conversation, try a bookshop.

♥ If you want elegant, confident and rich try Paul Smith.

♥ If you want a man who's good with his hands, try the local DIY shop.

By the time you've both walked in the door you've already got **something** in common, so you just need to get chatting. Ask him if he'd recommend Alex Garland or John Grisham. Ask him if you can hold a shirt up against him (your **brother** has the same colouring – make it clear you're not attached). Ask him for advice on the best kind of screw. It's easy! I promise.

Puppy Power
This works just as well for women as it does for men. Borrow a dog, find a park, and get out there!

Shopping (3)
This might sound a strange one, but try carrying lots and lots of carrier-bags, preferably precariously stuffed with fruit, veg and – most importantly – condoms. Once you're loaded up with your bag, you've got two possible options:

♥ Wait for a sexy bloke to offer to carry your groceries for you – an ideal opportunity to get talking

♥ The more pro-active approach: target yourself at the object of your affection and 'clumsily' walk into him so that your groceries spill all over the pavement. Not only will he be mortified at his mistake and keen to make it up to you (yum!) but, if your bag has split in the desired fashion, the condoms should prompt a frisson of sexual tension between you. Well, it worked in the ad so it's worth a try.

The Helpless Female
OK, perhaps not very politically correct, but a great way for women to get talking to men.

♥ If you've got a car, stand by it with the bonnet up, looking confused.

♥ Hang around in the middle of the street looking a bit vague until a sexy bloke comes along and then ask him directions – but make sure you're asking to go in the same direction as him, so you can walk together.

♥ Ask to borrow someone's mobile phone to make an urgent (but quick) call.

Admittedly these tactics aren't for everybody, but in extreme circumstances they're worth a try!

So the key to meeting a mate is to be broadminded. Get yourself in the right frame of mind (with a bit of visualisation), get your kit right, and go for it! And remember that dating opportunities can arise at the strangest times, so keep your eyes open!

Jenny – who you're probably beginning to feel you know very well – is the perfect example of the necessity to stay alert to every mating and dating opportunity. She was recently passing through a coffee shop and saw two rather delicious men – tree surgeons, it seemed from their overalls and the logo on their T-shirts – having a quiet lunch. She didn't waste any time but approached them to complain about her roots (her trees, not her hair) and asked whether they could tend to them. She quickly handed over her business card – to the one she most fancied, of course – and will no doubt get a call.

So what's the connection between soldiers, tree surgeons and City boys? The connection is this: Jenny keeps her eyes open. OK not all her plans work, but it's better to be broad-minded than to miss the opportunities right there under your nose. Don't not go to a party because you know your friend's friends and don't really get on with them. Grit your teeth and go anyway. Who's to say what the friends of your friend's friends are like? Think ahead. I know a girl who managed to meet her boyfriend in a lifeboat on a Greek island ferry. Don't ask.

Saturday Night
at the Movies
OR
First Date Protocol

This is the bridge too far, the eagle landing, the penalty shoot-out at the World Cup Final. In short, the first date is your one chance to get it right.

Do not mess up!

Not that I want to put the pressure on or anything . . .

This is not the time for tasteless jokes, extreme right-wing views, bad breath or white socks. It is, after all, so easy to get so many things so very wrong. Your stomach is doing somersaults, your legs have gone all wobbly and you're too jittery to string a sensible sentence together.

And what makes it worse is that you're wanting it to be a great success. Your body is a sea of hormones – IN A FORCE TEN GALE! However, in so far as it's remotely possible, be sensible. Don't, for instance, follow in the footsteps of one young man of my acquaintance.

> Matt met up with his mindblowingly sexy potential girlfriend and discovered, much to his amazement, that

she fancied the pants off him. In his excitement, he drank so much to calm his raging nerves that he ended up puking in the car next to her. It's an incident not easily forgotten, let alone picked out of the upholstery. Suffice to say that she never called him.

So TAKE YOUR DATE SERIOUSLY! If you don't want to mess up follow the simple rules below. It's easy once you know how . . .

CHECK YOUR LOOK

John Travolta in *Saturday Night Fever*. Madonna in *Desperately Seeking Susan*. The Fonz. What have they got in common? They've GOT THE LOOK. OK, so a few decades later shiny white suits, fingerless lacy gloves or a large greasy quiff might look a bit of a fashion faux-pas, but at the time John, Madonna and Fonzie were fashion gods. Now I'm not suggesting that you aspire to godlike status, but the point is that CLOTHES MATTER. Particularly on a first date.

Chances are that dater and datee have already met and have perhaps seen each other in a less than prepared state: drunk and dishevelled at closing time, for instance. Or, if you've been naughty, hungover and even more dishevelled first thing in the morning – let that be a lesson to you! No one can look glamorous, appealing, sexy or even alluringly wanton in that situation. You just look a mess and your breath smells.

Despite any such hiccups, the first date is your one chance to make an impression, and first impressions count. There's a piece of interview folklore that says an interviewer assesses a candidate within the first thirty seconds. Exactly the same thing applies to dates, because they are nothing less than an interview for the key role of *Partner*. Or *Other Half*. Or *Sex-Toy-Cum-Soul-Mate*. Whatever works for you. So you should not overlook the fact that you are wearing baggy neon-pink beach shorts, a white vest and scuffed biker boots. Nobody else will be able to overlook it – especially the shorts.

You'll inevitably want to look your best for your Big Night. If you're a girl you'll spend hours hanging around Marks & Spencer debating the relative merits of sheer, shiny and satin-finish tights (or suspenders if you're feeling frisky) in every conceivable shade. If you're a boy you'll hover suspiciously around the Men's Skincare range in Boots before buying a new razor, going home and cutting your face to ribbons with it. And whether you're a girl or a boy, you'll spend at least half an hour fretting over underwear options – Are these lacy knickers too porn-starry? Is this G-string too racy? Are these Y-fronts too grey? Are these lycra pants too nut-hugging?

But the most important thing is to wear something you feel natural in. There's no point putting on airs and graces and designer frocks if the next time your new date sees you you're wearing jeans and a T-shirt, and the frock is never seen again.

If you'll just allow me to indulge a pet obsession for a moment here, one thing I really can't stand is FAKES. I mean what on earth is the point? It's all very well trying to convince the man of your dreams that you're the girl of his, but if that involves feigning an interest in fox-hunting, beagling and walking tours of the Pennines when what you're really into is all-night clubbing, café society and ensuring that you're never more than spitting distance away from the nearest tube station, then what's the point? You might get the guy, or the girl, but you can't pretend for ever so when are you going to reveal your true self? The third date? Your one-year anniversary? When you get married? After your third son gets shipped off to boarding school at the age of four? It's stupid, so don't do it.

Now, back to clothes.

Gorgeous but not girly

The same rules apply to first dates as to going out to meet a mate – but a first date definitely takes more thought. Be sure to wear something appropriate – if you're going somewhere swanky, then feel free to dress up. Don't go for the Sporty Spice look if he's taking you to dinner at the Ivy and then on to the ballet. But don't wear the cocktail dress if you're going to watch Arsenal play or planning a picnic in the park. Don't wear stilettos and a mini-skirt to a theme park. Your heels will sink into the mud and every ten-year-old boy in the place (they have Girl Radar by that age) will gather beneath you every time you go on a ride, eager to catch a furtive glimpse of your knickers. Go casual. Go appropriate.

And one little tip, girls – don't dress too revealingly. You might think that plunge top and a belt for skirt makes you look sexy, but it doesn't. It makes you look tarty, and that's another thing altogether. Not a good look. So don't go looking like someone who hangs around street corners. Save that for a private bedroom-moment later in your relationship.

Beautiful boys

As for you blokes, you've really got it easy! Men have much less to worry about when it comes to their kit. Not only have you got less choice – I'm guessing most of you don't dither about whether to wear a flirty, frilly skirt or a slinky dress on a first date (although maybe later) – but there are fewer danger signals that men's clothes can send out. There are only really four absolute no-nos:

♥ STONE-WASHED JEANS are never an acceptable fashion statement

♥ STRING VESTS are social death

♥ WHITE SOCKS = wipe-out

♥ SUPER-TIGHT T-SHIRTS do not flatter. Not on even the most wonderful, chiselled, pumped and toned body. They look silly. Do you hear me? Silly.

Other than that, the rules are simple. Don't wear a suit if you're going to a bar or the cinema – you'll look like her bodyguard. Worse still, if you drive you'll look like her chauffeur. But on the other hand it's important that you show you've made an effort – she's not going warm to you if she's bothered to make herself look delicious and you turn up in your favourite old football-and-pub-with-the-boys clothes. Save the scruffbag side of you for later. Much later.

While there's often the odd particular look that really does it for some women – I personally find nice old T-shirts and worn jeans utterly irresistible, for instance – most men wear clothes to stop them being naked. And given the shape of most men, that's not an entirely bad thing.

The trendy trap
A final fashion tip for both guys and girls. Don't dress over-fashionably and end up looking like you've just stumbled out

of a Vogue shoot – not, at least, if your date isn't the hippest person on the planet.

A particularly gorgeous friend of mine, Tara, recently went out on a date with a man (Harry) she met in the park – they'd got chatting, found they had lots in common, fancied each other something rotten and decided to meet up again for dinner the next week. Tara had been wearing her lazy Sunday afternoon kit when they first met, but as Harry was particularly delicious she decided to go all-out to impress him. She's a pretty cool chick generally speaking, but in her excitement she went a bit overboard and turned up looking like a Catwalk Queen in spike-heeled strappy sandals, white pedal-pushers and a hot-pink checked busty gingham vest, all topped off with diamante hairclips and a Hello Kitty plastic pink handbag. Harry, who turned out to be a great bloke but not a fashion-head, was absolutely knocked sideways. And not in a good way. I mean sure, he thought she looked gorgeous, but she also looked like an Extremely Scary Person. They sat through dinner in virtual silence because Harry was convinced he had nothing to say that would interest this extraordinary vision. And it was only through the intervention of fate – her spiked heel snapped off as they left the restaurant and she went arse-over-tit into the street and they both collapsed into peals of nervous giggles – that they ended up ever seeing each other again. And now? They're about to move in together, actually, but Tara's well aware that she nearly blew it – fashion that's so cutting-edge it hurts can be way too intimidating for your average male.

GETTING READY

Whatever your look, make sure you give yourself the maximum time necessary to get ready, but not a minute longer or you'll either put yourself through a million costume changes, or you'll end up looking like a prize poodle. Done up, yes. Polished, for sure. But you'll still look like a dog. I can get ready for most things in a matter of minutes but if I let it slip I end up taking two hours which end in a hideous outfit and floods of tears.

A little hiccup

Talking of tears, women should also pay heed to the possible consequences of dating when suffering from PMT. Personally, for four days every month I am not a normal person, but a seething mess of irrationality and insecurity. I'm capable of only two possible extremes:

♥ utter collapse into a ball of trembling, mumbling neurosis OR

♥ a raging torrent of pent-up frustration.

And I find that neither approach creates a very good impression. Answering the question 'What would you like to drink?' with either 'I don't know – what do you think I should have?' or 'What's it to you?' tends not to get me very far.

Men need to keep this in mind. Of course you can't expect to be psychic, and even in these theoretically open-minded times asking a potential datee when they'll be PMT-free is a hard and somewhat intimate conversation if you haven't reached first-date yet, but if your date appears to be a little mad, it may not be her fault. (This, I should add, is an attitude which I applaud and could well be adopted more generally in regards to women.) That said, if she appears to be acting only a *little* oddly it may well not be PMT; perhaps she just doesn't like you much after all.

Of course on the plus side, women tend to subconsciously want to show off more flesh when they're ovulating. It's all part of that deep-seated biological effort to reel the man in. And, as any woman knows, it doesn't take much flesh on show to reel a man in.

Getting it Just Right

Back to getting ready: it's best to simply try and stress your best bits. Most women I know have a bit of a tummy fetish. I know that girl in *Pulp Fiction* went on about how sexy pot bellies are, but I defy you to find a real-life girl who aims for a pot belly when getting dressed for a date. Chances are you'll eat *something* while you're out, so if you're prone to sticky-out-stomach-syndrome don't go for an outfit that shows it off.

Similarly, if you feel comfortable in heels then wear those. But don't wear them if you spend most of your life in trainers. Your legs might look longer, but you'll end up tottering along like an injured giraffe. Besides, if you've got legs like mine, stressing them is probably not a brilliant idea. If other people have bad hair days and big nose syndrome, I have bad leg days and fat knee syndrome.

Remember also that not keeping your hot-spots – i.e. your best features – covered carries a certain price. If your boobs really are something to see and you choose to stress them, don't be surprised if your date spends most of the evening transfixed by them. Men can't help it. Try as they might to resist, breasts just draw them in – they're man-magnets. This is fine if you don't want him to know what colour eyes you have by the end of the evening – or even, in extreme cases, what colour your hair is – but it's hardly an aid to good conversation. The choice is yours. It's not hard to turn a man into a walking erection, so if you dress overtly sexily, don't take offence at the reaction you get. Of course I'm not saying that men shouldn't do their best to be polite and avert the eyes – staring's rude, boys, however nice the view – but drawing attention to your best bits does just that: draw attention to your best bits.

Basically, I reckon there are three ways to dress: sexy, dowdy and Just Right. And it's finding that Just Right that's not easy. A good tip is to get a mate round to help you choose the right outfit. This has three advantages:

♥ She can tell you what works and what makes you look like a pig as you spend two hours trawling through every item in your wardrobe.

♥ It's a good laugh.

♥ Your mate can be there to meet your new date when he or she arrives, thus providing you with an objective, third-party assessment.

But listen to her opinion! It's easy to be so blinded by love and/or lust that you miss some screamingly obvious problem: that he's psychopathic or she's cruel to animals, for instance. Flaws like these might pass you by, but they won't escape the beady eye of your friend.

This is why the friend who comes round has to be female. Women have scarily acute powers of observation – at least they're acute when it comes to looking someone up and down and decoding every last detail. In two minutes women are able to tell whether a man is a gentleman (from his behaviour), whether he's kind (from his eyes), what tribe he belongs to (from his dress), how open and honest he is (by the way he gets on with her), and also pick up a weighty tome of other insights from his body-shape, hair, face and, above all, his shoes. Are his shoes clean and unsecured? Has he made the effort? Such details are important.

Ask a man what a woman was like and you'll get some incisive comment like 'she was nice' or, worse still, 'she had nice breasts'. But where a man notices curves, a woman picks up on personality – far more helpful. Which is why a good mate who's female is as essential for a man as it is for a woman.

Women can assess other women just as effectively as they assess men – we've got the same (or similar) hormones rushing around inside our bodies. A good girl friend is of inestimable use to the bachelor in separating off the fluffy, girly girls who will drive you nuts within a month, the leeches who'll never let go once they've sucked a man's blood, and the oh-so-selfish career types from the fun-loving, independent, secure girls you lovely men deserve to be with. We can spot the ones you shouldn't go near a mile off:

♥ girls who say 'it's really weird, all my best friends are boys' and sound really proud

♥ girls who only talk to other girls if they think they can get them introduced to someone they fancy

♥ girls who look over your shoulder in a conversation

THESE ARE NOT NICE GIRLS. And there's often a fine line between nice and nasty, one that can only be detected by another woman. It's like pigs and truffles. And you don't want to end up with a mushroom when you could have a delicacy!

Check Your Pits

I can't stress enough that every pore on your body should be Clean Clean Clean. If you were an ad, it would be for washing powder. You have to dazzle with cleanliness.

Personally, the very first impression I have of someone is often determined by their smell. I'm sure I'm not alone in being horribly overcome by bad body smells – and, for that matter, over-zealous attempts to mask those smells. Three gallons of after-shave or perfume and six roll-on deodorant blocks may make you comfortable with your own aroma, but for those around you it's going to be like spending an evening in a chemical refinery. There is of course the school of thought that believes that a slightly sweaty man smells sexy – those pheromones get the hormones buzzing – but it's really all a question of location. Slightly sweaty is acceptable if you've just got in from a run, or you've just dug a trench. Being slightly sweaty and, what is worse, *smelling* slightly sweaty isn't ideal if you're just standing there. Being a prop in a game of rugby is hard work. Propping up the bar is not.

Similarly, smelly breath is the kiss of death to clinch-potential. It's certainly the kiss of death to kissing. My three indispensable tips are:

1. **Floss regularly**

2. **Use an electric toothbrush**

or, if you don't fancy 1. and 2.:

3.   Don't open your mouth within three feet of your date.

Option 3. obviously puts a downer on getting too intimate and probably means that all conversation will have to be shouted. It certainly makes the kind of head-to-head conversation required in many loud bars and clubs next to impossible. But don't say I didn't warn you.

Going too far

One last point. Hygiene is all very well, but reasonable hygiene doesn't include taking your toothbrush and a clean set of underwear with you. Although you may do this in all innocence – just slipping a spare pair of undies into your bag or your coat pocket either by accident or out of force of habit with no hidden agenda whatsoever (yeah, right!) – if you're found out it gives a very bad impression. Should your date extend beyond the boundaries of a pleasant evening into a dangerous night, then don't lord it up with the Aquafresh next morning. It's way too easy for anyone to read between the lines and see that either:

♥ You assumed your date was going to be an easy lay. And even though the night's events have proven your guess to be true, that doesn't warrant rubbing it in. OR

♥ You do this all the time, which may or may not be true, but given your packing foresight is likely to be the latter. And even if the latter *is* true, you don't necessarily want to broadcast the fact.

Just go with the flow. Don't turn up with your overnight bag and your face-cream.

JUDGE AND JURY

I know first impressions matter, but try not to be too judgemental. Bear in mind that, like you, your date is probably a bag of nerves. Performing dog routines and all manner of party tricks come out of the crumbly old wood-work on first dates, and they are not necessarily representative of the way a person really is when you've got to know them.

> My friend Alan once spent an entire first date (admittedly it was a blind date, so even more nerve-racking) churning out a string of *Blues Brothers*, *Withnail and I* and *Star Wars* gags and quotes. Not his usual style, I hasten to say, but he was very very nervous, and his date wasn't a great talker. He was mortified afterwards, but screwed up the courage to ask her out again. And she said no. She lost out. He's an absolute sweetheart, and she can't have seen the real Alan at all.

People say and do dumb things that they don't mean, because first dates are scary. People are guarded, showy, stressed, cocky, shy, quiet and arrogant all at the same time. So be prepared to give it a second shot if there was even a twinkling of a glint of a spark of something between you.

Remember that a little mutual understanding can go a very long way. Too much mutual understanding can go all the way.

THE DATE

There are zillions of golden rules for getting the first date right, but numero uno is:

Don't set up false expectations
(Please will those men who think that throwing large wads of £50 notes at their date is a good idea take note!)

Of course there *are* gold-diggers out there (easy to spot because they're the twenty-year-olds with large breasts and multi-millionaire septuagenarian husbands), but whatever men may think, it's absolutely a myth that most women are impressed by money. What do you think we are? Stupid? (Don't answer that)

And there's another problem: flexing the gold card on a first night out might well backfire at a later date. We all like a treat, but if a girl goes out on a first date with a man who turns up in a Porsche waving two dozen roses and then proceeds to feed her Krug, caviar and lobster, she'll come to certain conclusions about him. If the man turns up next time in an old jalopy and hasn't shaved because he couldn't afford a pack of razors, then she might just suspect that their first encounter was a bit of a hollow performance. What makes a date exciting is to make it unusual. Doing something slightly mad – certainly something that you or your date would never normally do – is a great way of breaking the ice.

To take an extreme example, you might go jet-skiing before you eat. Even if you hate water, have a long-established fear of speeds and look terrible in a wetsuit, at least it will build up your appetite! Think positive!

But if you're the one choosing what to do, be careful what

you select for it will surely come back to haunt you.

- ♥ Don't make like you're a jet-skiing expert if you've never done it before and wouldn't be caught dead in the water without your arm-bands

- ♥ Don't come over as all arty and literary by suggesting a poetry reading if the closest you come to poetry is Oasis lyrics. When your date sees that your small bookshelf contains nothing but dog-eared Barbara Cartlands or pulp SAS blockbusters, they'll see through you. I guarantee it. And they *won't* be pleased.

- ♥ Don't take your date to the ballet or the opera if as soon as they see your home – and your CD collection – they'll realise you're a thrash metal freak. You won't have impressed them, you'll have them thinking you need to be sedated. (Actually, that applies to thrash metal freaks generally)

A good friend of mine (who shall, for the sake of his pride and our friendship remain nameless) managed to get a date with the girl of his dreams. He'd always fancied her, but never had the nerve to speak to her. He finally managed to screw up the (Dutch) courage, and asked her out on a date. To his utter surprise and delight she said yes, but of course he was then faced with the worst dilemma of all: he had to take her somewhere. And this wasn't just any girl, this was the *perfect* girl. It clearly had to be the perfect date. He'd overheard her saying she liked shellfish, and therefore decided that shellfish it had to be. The best. So he took her out for the perfect, sublime shellfish experience, and that's what it was. For her, anyway. Unfortunately, he'd never eaten shellfish before so the meal didn't start particularly well: he began by gagging on his oysters, and then moved on to trying to eat prawns with their shells on. By the time he'd sent a lobster claw flying into her lap, he knew things were really not going well. They got worse. He hadn't allowed for the possibility that not only might he not like shellfish, but it might not like him. It didn't. The oysters, prawns, lobster and God knows what else had a big fight in his stomach, and landed on the pavement outside the restaurant. It was not a good date.

So you mustn't choose something that might disagree with you rather violently, but you equally well can't choose something that might prove insensitive. That's *not* a date. For example, men, generally, shouldn't try to take women to the football. Or on a regular lager-and-curry Friday-night-with-the-lads. Or to the finals of Miss World, even though you've got front-row seats. Especially if you have front-row seats.

A good happy medium is often doing something exciting and out of the ordinary. And if things are going really badly, it will give you something to talk about, which can be very useful sometimes – believe me! I once (in my earlier match-making days, before I was as adept at it as I am now) made the mistake of setting up two rather shy and retiring friends on a blind date. *They're similar*, I thought. *They'll understand one another*, I thought.

I thought wrong!

My girlfriend phoned the next day in floods of tears, to tell me that it was the worst experience of her life. Other than ordering food and talking about the weather, neither of them had said a word. Now if they'd gone jet-skiing first, I bet they wouldn't have had a problem finding something to talk about!

You needn't be as extravagant as that, of course. You could go on an open-air bus tour (I've always wanted to do that), go for a cycle-ride, visit the zoo (one of my personal favourites, and gets girls in a suitably flirty frame of mind – I think it's all the baby animals, they make us broody), play some pool – whatever grabs you. Whatever might be a new – or at least not everyday – experience for one of you.

But if you want a more traditional date, here are some indispensable guidelines.

Table for Two
If you're out to dinner, there are some basic rules to follow.

Avoid:

- ♥ foods that include tomato sauces – with all your nerves you're guaranteed to get more down your front than in your mouth

- ♥ pasta (the ideal culinary launch-pad for tomato sauce)

- ♥ garlic and onions (even if you have no intention of kissing, both smells linger)

- ♥ lettuce, especially the frilly variety that goes up your nose (if lettuce is unavoidable, cut it into small pieces – don't try and fold it into your face like some bizarre oral origami)

♥ any avant-garde food – that's all food you've not tried before – should also be avoided. Don't risk a bad reaction and violent stomach upsets later that evening.

On the plus-side, hot-dogs are good, not only for their obvious suggestive quality when eaten, but also because they allow you to lick your fingers afterwards, which is even more effective, I find.

And girls – ABANDON YOUR DIETS! Don't even *think* about pushing a carrot around your plate for an hour. Healthy eating is all very well, but an enthusiastic appetite is an attractive thing in a woman (shows signs of being a good breeder, you see). Or rather, no appetite or obsessing about one's figure isn't sexy. And trying to look enthusiastic about something even a rabbit would consider to be a pre-dinner snackette will just draw attention to your weight paranoia.

Once you've got your food, remember not to eat noisily or talk with your mouth full – having to dodge a fusillade of semi-chewed chunks as they rocket out of someone's mouth is not fun and definitely not heart-warming – and at the end of each course, slope off to check your teeth for unwanted bits. If your companion fails to do this and is bit-encrusted, do tell them. They may be momentarily embarrassed, but they won't be pleased to get home at the end of the date to find that half of their starter has been lodged defiantly and boldly between their front teeth, turning their normally dazzling smile into that of Long John Silver.

If you're in a posh restaurant and find the armoury of cutlery you're presented with a little baffling, be honest about it. Don't try and bluff it by confidently holding forth your water glass when the waiter goes to pour your wine – or getting upset when he only pours enough for a teetotal squirrel into your glass (he's offering it to you to taste, dummy). It's far better to play it straight and just make a joke of it. But if you're choosing the restaurant, don't go for somewhere you'll be out of your depth – then you *will* look silly. However, just for the record I'd like to say that I was horrified when one girlfriend of mine returned after a date and announced that her companion had a bad case of HKLP – that's 'Holds Knife Like Pen' – something she found, completely unacceptable. HSCYG! (How superficial can you get)

Finally, go easy on the alcohol! As my friend Matt's experience suggests, it can lead to disaster and, frankly, collapsing head-first into your creamed spinach will do your romantic credibility no good at all. And of course it's always useful to actually *remember* the date when trying to decide if you want to repeat the experience. Although it's tempting to have a quick shot to calm you down, avoid drinking before you meet. Not only will you always be one step ahead, but your breath will smell – even vodka smells. Besides, going into a date raw is by far the best way. Feel the fear and relish it anyway!

A Spot of Lunch

Lunch is sometimes a better option than dinner – it's much more relaxed, so the pressure's off in every way. It's much less scary to invite someone out to lunch because if you get turned down it's not like you asked for a *date*, so surely even the most feeble girl can get 'why don't we meet for lunch?' into an animated conversation. And if your conversation isn't animated, I have no idea why you want to date this person.

Once you get to The Big Day, getting ready is much simpler – it's way easier to decide what to wear to lunch as you know it's going to be fairly casual. No suits or flowing frocks here, thank you very much. It's also much easier for the dater to choose somewhere to take the datee: choose a really nice pub that does great food. Personally I'm a great fan of The Thatcher House in Ravenscourt Park – great food, relaxed atmosphere, busy enough to be lively but never a scrum. I'll admit it's not terribly convenient if you don't live in west London though.

Other pluses of a pub lunch include:

- ♥ you can have a sociable drink beforehand, then decide how many courses you want once you get a feel for whether you want to make it a leisurely meal or get the hell out of there

- ♥ you don't have to eat as much, so sticky-out-stomach-syndrome is less of an issue

- ♥ you're unlikely to drink as fast at lunchtime so the old not-remembering-the-end-of-the-date thing is less of a worry

- ♥ it's bound to be cheaper – without *seeming* cheap – than a posh dinner

- ♥ it's perfectly acceptable to only spend a couple of hours at lunch if things get tricky – and no-one's embarrassed

- ♥ and if things get *really* terrible, you can almost pretend it wasn't a date anyway – just two friends meeting up for an unusually quiet, surprisingly short lunch

But if things go well, it's perfect. Lunch can go as long as you like, and you're free to spend the afternoon together. If you're getting on well – and if you're still there lingering over your third coffee at half-past four then I promise you're getting on well – it's perfectly natural to suggest a trip to the park to walk off your lunch, or you could progress to a film. Hell, if things go really well you can spend the evening together.

I've even convinced myself. A lazy, leisurely, relaxed lunch is the way forward.

The Flicks

But if you're off your food, the cinema is the other classic date destination, and with very good reason. It's intimate – you're in the dark and you're usually sitting close to one another (unless you arrive late and end up a few rows apart which wouldn't make for a very good date at all), and you get to share things like popcorn and, of course, that suggestive hot-dog again.

But be careful about your choice of film. Anything featuring zombie flesh-eaters, graphic blood-shed and/or Jean-Claude Van Damme is probably best avoided. It will put you off your popcorn. If the bloke is picking, anything too manly – guns, explosions, no plot, ridiculous villains, little green men, outer space etc. – is probably not on. She'll possibly hate it, and even if she doesn't, there'll be a niggling little voice at the back of her mind telling her you didn't exactly consider her when choosing the film. But anything too girlie is also out – women in trauma, bonding, sisterhood etc. She'll either think you're a wuss, or she'll think you're just pandering to what you imagine her tastes to be, that you're trying too hard to present yourself as a New Man. And she'll be right.

That doesn't leave much. Suspenseful films, however, at least mean you have a great excuse for grabbing one another, a feat someone I know managed to pull off in *There's Something About Mary*, a slap-stick comedy. But she was a very good actress and obviously very easily surprised. Romantic films will get you in the right mood, but they might be the cinematic equivalent of coming on too strong, and anything with graphic sex scenes is definitely a no-no. Such films are usually reserved for couples – and you, remember, are not yet a couple. You'll just have to watch it together when it comes out on video.

One more thing – don't even think of sitting in the back row. That's way too cutesy. Any fool will see through that a mile off. And let's hope for your sake you're not wasting all this energy on a fool.

Painting the Town Red

Bars and clubs might be fine for meeting people, but they're really not good for a first date. A quiet bar has its charm, especially if you know the staff and can play the celebrity for a few hours, but a quiet bar is, one might suspect, not a very good bar. And anywhere that's packed is just not on – especially if it's likely to be packed with people you know. You'll only end up spending half the evening talking to them, and that won't make you very popular with your date.

More to the point, big crowds are not conducive to getting to know each other. Shouting at each other over some German minimalist hard-core techno while having an over-priced drink spilled on you by someone in a sweaty T-shirt is, frankly, not my idea of a romantic evening. And while a man who can dance really well is sexy, he is also a rarity. Men all too inevitably embarrass themselves on the dancefloor with those funny, jerky movements that make them look like they're having a minor seizure or someone's just stuck something pointy up their bottom. It's not an attractive sight. Compare this disaster-inducing venue to a moonlit walk by a river. Which would you rather do with someone you really really fancy? Which one is least likely to involve moonwalking?

The other problem with bars and clubs is the drinking thing – or more specifically the drinking and NO FOOD thing. Even the best of us, with the strongest stomachs, can succumb to the curse of drinking on an empty stomach and end up either dancing on a table to *Borderline* (and yes, we really *do* think we sound like Madonna), or picking a fight with the nearest bloke on account of the fact that he was 'looking at me funny'. And neither of these is a good thing. Particularly not on a first date. They're not always a great thing when you're just out with your mates (particularly the fighting bit, as the bloke whose cross-eyed, blurry stare you object to so strongly is probably in fact your best friend), but on a first date they're Very Bad. And on a first date, with butterflies jitterbugging around your stomach, it's very easy to drink faster than you usually do. Dancing butterflies, drinking and no food are a terrible combination. Take my word for it.

If Music Be the Food of Love . . .

This is a slightly tricky one, and definitely not something to spring on a datee you don't know well. Because if you take them to a gig and the music's not to their taste, you're faced with Definite Disaster. Personally, I'd rather carve my name on my arm with a compass than go to see Bon Jovi live. So if you're going to surprise your date with tickets to the concert of their dreams – ask first.

But once you've got over that little hurdle, a concert can be a great date. There's not too much pressure because you don't have to make conversation *all* the time, but you'll find it's easy to chat when you're both revved up about the music. There's a great atmosphere, everyone's totally excited, and you can jump around loads – which gives you the opportunity to bounce into each other a lot and make that all-important physical contact. Plus, a great concert is a guaranteed good time, so you've got a better chance of making it to the second date. It's hard to decide you don't like someone when you're moving in rhythm.

The Dinner Party

Maybe this is cheating a bit, but if you really can't face that First Date, then you could try having a dinner party. This is a particularly good bet if you live with friends, as you can each invite one person you fancy. It's not exactly a date, but the way the couples are supposed to pair off will be pretty obvious, and it's quite a rejection-free route to take as few people say no to a dinner party.

If it all goes horribly wrong you've got your mates there to get pissed with and you'll all have a good time. But if it goes well, it's an intimate enough atmosphere for you to have a proper one-on-one conversation and find out if you really like each other. And if things go *really* well, you can retire to the sofa to find out lots more about each other . . .

But if you're planning a dinner, there are a few things to remember:

♥ Try to keep it down to eight people – four couples. Otherwise you'll all end up shouting and there's no room for an intimate chat

♥ If your Sainsbury's trolley is usually full of pasta sauce and microwaveable meals, don't try and whip up a gourmet dinner. You'll just give yourself a nervous breakdown. Go for something you know you can cook (and make sure your mum's on the other end of the phone line for quick emergency tips)

♥ Try and finish cooking at least an hour or so before you've told people to arrive. Just because you're having people round to your home doesn't mean you don't need to Check Your Look. And your pits.

♥ Make sure there's lots of wine, but get some water in too. And drink it! You won't keep it up for long, but if you at least *start* by drinking a glass of water to every glass of wine you'll be less likely to drop the pudding.

I know four blokes who used to live together at university. A few weeks after they'd moved into their student house (a tip, I should mention), they decided to experiment with having a dinner party so they invited four girls. And, remarkably, it all went completely according to plan. David shelled some prawns and mixed them up with thousand island dressing. Ben called his mum and got a blow-by-blow guide to roasting a chicken. Robin – bizarrely – knew how to make syllabub. And Jon – well, Jon set the table. It was a strange meal, and not necessarily a gourmet one, but it did the trick. The four girls were so impressed by the trouble their hosts had gone to – and their apparent domestic skills – that two out of four ended up dating David and Robin. The fact that they were intended for

83

Ben and Jon is irrelevant. It worked, didn't it! The boys went on to have a dinner party per term – I suspect they weren't looking for long-term relationships! – and they were all similarly successful. Except the one where they all got food poisoning, but that's another story.

One point though. If you've invited someone to dinner, then it's definitely *them* who has to arrange the next date. When they say thanks for the lovely evening, don't storm in here with 'It was great, wasn't it. Can I take you out for dinner on Wednesday?' – that's their job.

LET'S TALK

A sexual buzz is great. It's fantastic. And there's often a lovely frisson between two strangers on a first date. After all you're there to decide whether you want – either in the short or long term but at some point – to have sex with each other. But however strong the sexual tension is, you'll just feel tense unless you can talk to one another. That's not to say you've got to get deeply personal – though obviously if you feel comfortable telling each other your life stories in intimate detail, or confiding your deepest, darkest fears and fantasies, then that's either a very good sign that you're destined for each other or a very good sign that you need a therapist. And that's useful to know as well.

Conversation isn't always easy. I'm never short of a word or ten thousand but not everyone is as talkative as me. Some people are quiet types. At least I think they're quiet types. Maybe they just couldn't get a word in edgeways.

Conversation needn't be about trying to beat a world record, but it *does* have to be two-way. Nothing is worse than being trapped with someone who talks endlessly about themselves. You might learn a lot about them, but one of the things you learn will be that you never want to see them again. At least not unless you can take a Walkman or a good book with you.

A word of warning though. There are some topics that should not be discussed, no matter how well you seem to be getting on:

♥ **DO** talk about each other, your interests, your families, aspects of your lives that overlap, places you've been, places you'd like to go, what you do with your days.

♥ **DON'T** talk about any of the above too much. You want to be interesting, and as fascinating as the intricate detail of your daily grind at the office is to you, your date is unlikely to want to know about the quirks of your photocopier. Similarly, you may love your dog, cat or goldfish passionately, and it may be important to you that a Life Partner shares your passion, but you can't really expect someone else to get all hot and bothered about an animal they've never even met. However snuffly, fluffy or scaly it is.

♥ **DON'T** have a scoresheet. It's not fair to write someone off just because they start talking about something you wouldn't do if you were paid. Keep an open mind.

Oh, but there are a couple of things which entitle you to write someone off. If your date starts advocating White Supremacy, praising the BNP or lecturing you on how a woman's place is in the kitchen, it's entirely acceptable (and indeed advisable) to walk out.

♥ **DON'T** talk about your intimate sexual preferences – you'll definitely end up in bed and you want to end up in bed because your *head* tells you to – not just because you've spent the last two hours listening to someone you might not actually terribly like tell you about all the amazing things they'd like to do to you (on which subject, I should point out that women no longer fall for it when men eulogise about how much they love giving head. We know you just say it because it's what we want to hear).

♥ **DON'T** talk about your exes – unless it's to say what a terrible time you had with them and how you still haven't found real love, sob. And even then, there are limits to how much you want to share about your disastrous love life. Go on too long, and they'll think you're either mad or desperate.

♥ **DON'T** talk about marriage or children – you want to seduce them, not scare them to death

♥ **DON'T** talk about religion, unless it's Christmas, and even then you should stick to the nativity.

THE TEN YEAR CV

Full time position: boy/girlfriend. Must have experience. Good package. Special concerns: love and sex. Terms negotiable. Long hours.

OK, so you can't be blatant about it, but what you *should* talk about is the ten-year CV. Be subtle, but what you're looking for is this:

- ♥ He/she needs to have had at least one longterm relationship (long-term being over six months)
- ♥ If he/she hasn't had one long-term relationship, they should have a very good reason why not – a career in the secret service, time in prison, he/she's been living on a remote island.
- ♥ Check their career/education path, as commitment to some consistent course of action reflects an ability to commit to a relationship. If he/she has flitted between painting and decorating, nursing, sky-diving and shoe-selling, they might have some great stories to tell, but won't be likely to go long term with you.

And one crucial extra tip for girls: find out whether the new man in your life gets on his mother. **Seriously.** If a man has a good relationship with his mum, then he's capable of having a good relationship with you. He might not want to, but at least he's capable. A man's ability to relate to all women will be shaped by his relationship by his mother. This is why children sent off to single-sex boarding schools grow up with such weird ideas about the opposite sex, and behave in such a gauche, cack-handed way in their presence. It's not embarrassment. It's because they haven't worked out quite what you are.

Guys – check what her relationship with her father is. The same thing applies.

Once you've got a bit further than first date, try to meet the mother or father as soon as possible. You can pretty much guarantee that if they're good, even people, then your date will have a good chance of being a nice person. Children learn bad habits and deep-seated fears from their parents – it's like seeing a mother pull her toddler away from dogs in the park because she is scared of dogs. The toddler grows up scared of dogs. So remember that you don't want a partner who won't chuck a bone for Fido.

Whatever you do, wherever you go, whatever you talk about, there's one thing to remember: *if you enjoyed yourself, say so*. Don't keep it a secret. This should really go without saying – but that's the problem: so many of us do go without saying.

EMERGENCY EXIT

Romance isn't easy. It doesn't always work out as planned. We change our minds and make mistakes. Sometimes, we wake up with them too.

Dumping

Getting out of a date can be as hard as getting one in the first place and the fact of the matter is that there is no easy way to do it. So you don't have to be blunt, but you do have to be straight.

For example, say you've given your number to someone who – at some point on some evening in some bar – you had some reason to fancy somewhat. None of it is very clear to you. But you're ex-directory, and there he is on the phone, asking you out. It's all a bit fuzzy. He's already had to describe himself to jog your memory – humiliating in itself – and finally the mist is clearing. Oh yes, he was the one with what you thought was a cool goatee like that bloke from Jamiroquai, but which you now suspect was actually just some nasty stubble. And he was temping as a morgue attendant so he smelt a bit odd, but you'd had a horrible day and at least he listened to you, so that was a good thing. And of course *he* was the one who'd had all those disastrous relationships – you're sure you remember him explaining how he goes to counselling four times a week about his rejection complex – so in your tipsy state you didn't want to be responsible for pushing him over the edge. OK, so he's a disaster area, but you have to be cruel to be kind. You know it's not going anywhere so the best thing to do is to tell him so. Tell him you're not ready, and tell him *now* rather than making a date and then spending the next four days trying to make a call to cancel, then chickening out and resorting to standing him up. Isn't it kinder to let him down now, than to send him off to wait for two hours in the pouring rain, having organised a discreet but fashionable table at one of those posh restaurants where they take your credit card details when you book? Of course it is.

Be honest – tell him you made a mistake. Just say 'no, not interested, thank-you'. Thank-you is always worth saying. But no is more important.

It's even harder when you've already had that first date, because it's much harder to pin down why there was no spark between you. Especially if you ended up in bed together. But if there was no vibe – you couldn't feel it calling in the air – you were all out of love – and your date calls to arrange another meeting, then tact and sensitivity are key. Don't go into detail. Don't start being picky about how you couldn't stand his white socks or his Terry Wogan haircut – the truly keen will merely respond by offering to go sock shopping or pop to the barber's right now. Just tell him you're sorry but it just wasn't right, or that you don't feel comfortable with it. It's not him. It's you. Even if it is him. Even if it is those socks.

It takes a bit more explaining, much more deviousness and considerably less honesty to get out of a date while it's happening. The best way – no matter how desperate the conversation is, no matter if you sit in funereal silence, no matter how badly you're getting on (well, if you're throwing punches you're probably within your rights to just get up, brush yourself down and go) – is just to bite the bullet and see it through to the bitter end.

If you want to make it clear things aren't working, keep your body language strictly platonic: don't touch, make minimum eye contact, consciously draw a mental boundary between you. This is certainly no time for honesty: extricating yourself mid-date with the announcement that it's all been a bit of a cock-up is tantamount to telling your companion that they're rubbish company. It's simply too cruel.

Other exit routines are not to be recommended, but I might as well fill you in on them so you'll know what to avoid.

♥ Develop a nervous tick – or start behaving utterly abominably – so that your date pulls the plug. I once had a date at my house – just sitting and chatting in the sitting room – and managed to fall asleep in front of him. When I woke up, he was gone and I never heard from him again.

♥ The second solution is considerably more underhand, but hey, it worked. So badly was the date going that I excused myself to go to the ladies, sneakily rang my friend and explained the situation. Ten minutes later, she rang me on my mobile with news of an unfortunate emergency that I just *had* to leave to sort out. Sorry. Gotta go. Bye. He never called either. And, ironically, I was mortified when he didn't.

♥ Of course the most severe option is waiting until your eager date goes to check his teeth, and then simply walking out. As I say, this is not something I recommend but if it's either that or stabbing yourself in the leg with your fork, then at least leave your share of the bill on the table.

Being Dumped

By the same token, you should be ready for rejection. Women usually expect a call within three days. Some are prepared to wait a week. Others, the truly desperate, will be all of a flutter whenever the phone rings six months later. Grow up! The fact is that if he is interested, he will call. And any wise man will simply call the next day. *Treat 'em mean, keep 'em keen* games don't work because *Treat 'em mean, say goodbye* is nearer the truth. And any person who claims they aren't ready to commit is a person who is lying. The harsh truth is that they aren't ready to commit to you. If the right person came along – Leonardo di Caprio or Winona Ryder, for instance – you could bet an awful lot they'd get over their commitment-phobia pretty sharpish. A no is a no. Don't pursue it. It's their loss, right?

But perhaps don't forget it totally: take the example of a friend of mine, Emily, who was in love with a friend of hers for ages. He knew how she felt, but could only ever see her as a mate. She would go out in a group

with him and his various girlfriends and he would come
to her for consolation when his relationships didn't
work out. And so on, for six years, her love for him
never faltering. And then one day the penny dropped.
He recognised that whenever he was down, she was
there for him, that she was utterly loyal and supportive,
that they stuck together through thick and thin. And
it's too Disney to believe, but he fell in love with her.
And now they're married. All together now: ahhh,
lovely.

FINAL MOMENTS

Assuming you haven't done a runner, there comes a moment
when the date has run its course and must come to its end.

WHAT NOW?

Naturally, if it's all been a disaster and you've sat there in
mutual silence for three hours – or you've sat in silence
while he filled you in on how when he was a
Fundamentalist Mormon he used to like to dress up in pink
rubber and be mildly electrocuted for kicks by his
wonderful, international catwalk model ex-wife – then the
only thing to say is thank-you and goodbye. But, as utter
disasters are (surprisingly) rare, you'll probably both be
frantically trying to decode the myriad signals you've been
exchanging throughout the date.

If he kept trying to get his hands down your pants all
evening, you'll know that he's at least interested in one thing.
If he stared into his coffee all night, chances are he simply isn't

interested in you. Sorry, but everyone needs some straight-talking once in a while.

But what if this one has been just perfect? Good talking, loads of jokes, little intimacies, shared interests and attitudes, lusty thoughts, the full Monty. Ideally – and I freely admit I'm a complete romantic – the man should escort the woman home. If he's a gentleman, as he would be in the perfect world, he will simply get you home safely, kiss you on the cheek, and say goodbye, glancing back one more time to check if the woman is still looking (which she will be if she's interested).

At this point, the parting words are all-important to prevent your new-found relationship from floundering in uncertainty. Assuming you're not a fan of floundering, one of you has to tell the other that they'll call – and if it looks like your date isn't going to say it, SAY IT INSTEAD. Go on! Be brave! But it's just as important to say *when* you're going to call – and then call when you said you would. There's a lot of rubbish talked about what key phrases like this mean, but it's really very simple:

- ♥ 'in a couple of days' means what it says: in two days

- ♥ 'in a few days' means in four or five days max

- ♥ 'soon' means in two or three days

- ♥ 'in a while' is a big kiss off (there's an ironic phrase for you)

- ♥ a simple 'I'll call' is also a kiss off

- ♥ if your date says 'Do give me a call' then the ball is placed firmly in your court. It's down to you to be clear with your intentions. Shame.

To kiss or not to kiss

Now this is the point at which you lovely readers will start to hate me – just until you see the blinding logic of my argument, I hope – because I'm afraid to say I'm not going to advise you to jump headlong into each other's arms, and from there into bed. Sorry.

If you're looking for a great one-night stand, a passionate shag with someone whose name (and possibly face) you'll never remember – although you might remember other parts of their anatomy – then go ahead. Close your eyes, part your lips, hope you've got your party pants on and go for it!

However, if you're looking for love – and I think we've established that that's what we're all after – hold your horses. And not because of some out-of-date morality but because this really isn't the best time to go for it. If you really like each other, if you're really going to have fantastic sex, it'll be better if you wait. I promise.

There's loads of rubbish talked about how the first time is always a let-down, and one *reason* it's a let-down is that you don't know each other. But if you wait until you understand each other a bit better, until you really like each other, until you can't sleep at night for wanting to get naked together, then you'll have mind-blowing sex. Honestly – I've tried it, and it works. And the same thing applies to kissing. Of course you don't have to hold out on the kissing thing for long – there's only so much will-power a person can be expected to have – but wait till after the first date. The suspense will be great and your first snog will be truly memorable.

Consider **Davina's Law of Relationship Length**: the longer the time between the first date and the first snog, the longer a relationship is likely to last. And consider this: the time before that first kiss is utterly magical, the time in which you get to explore each others' wants and needs before you start exploring each others' hot'n'hairy bits. It's a time that makes that first kiss absolutely monumental because you're kissing someone you really like. Call me an old romantic, but romance is what it's all about, after all.

So now I know it's tempting, girls – I've been there, on the doorstep, with all those lovely, warm, tingly feelings – but if you're after anything more than a quick shag don't invite him in for coffee. To the vast majority of men, you might as well strip all your clothes off, grab him by the crotch and tell him that the bed needs warming. Once he's inside, he's in your intimate space and you're revealing all manner of things to him. One of those things could end up being what you look like naked. However much you fancy him, it's really much better to make a clean break at the end of the first night – and to do this at the doorstep, not with your bra pushed up round your neck and your knickers hanging from one ankle. That's just not dignified. There's lots of time for getting up to naughty things later. I promise.

If you do make the mistake of letting your date slip through the front door and then decide you don't want to take things any further (well, you might be absolutely gagging to take it further but you've decided to wait so instead of ripping his clothes off you're counting the moments until that cold shower), then the best idea is, after the coffee, to start washing up the mugs and making noises about how you really must get to bed as you've got an early start the next day – and offer to see your date to the door. If he asks for a kiss, or to stay (which, let's be honest here, will amount to the same thing) just say no. However sweetly he asks, and however lovely his smile. Say no. Be firm. Even if he is.

NOT AN OFFICER, BUT AT LEAST A GENTLEMAN

Now listen carefully. I'm here to warn you about the near-extinction of one of my favourite species:

THE GENTLEMAN
Political correctness and ladettism have nearly wiped them out.

Yobs are not sexy. Louts are not sexy men. The kind of man who says 'get your coat, love, you've pulled' is most *definitely* not sexy. But what is sexy is a man who acts like a gentleman, especially on a first date. We may be independent women, but that doesn't mean we don't deserve to be spoilt. There's loads of room for women spoiling men as well – after all, part of the fun of being in love with someone is doing those cute little intimate things for them (no, I didn't mean *those* intimate things) – but in my book they come later. Not on a first date. And I don't mean anything too drastic, just little details.

> Years ago I had a friend who fell utterly in love with a man because he paid her bus fares. Now I know that sounds daft, and she's most definitely an independent career girl but, although we're only talking about the odd 50p here and there, the fact that he made little gestures like that, that he looked out for her, made her feel really special. She's living with him now.

Attention to details like this inevitably wear off after time, but that's no reason not to go that extra mile at the beginning of a relationship. Little touches like pouring her wine rather than waiting for her to help herself, opening the door for her (but don't trip her up in your rush to beat her to the door handle) are lovely. They allow the man to feel that he's in control, which appeals to his Alpha Maleness, but they are absolutely *not*, despite the popular misconception, an affront to women. Everyone likes to be spoilt sometimes, so don't deny yourself. We might be strong women, entirely self-sufficient in our day-to-day lives, well-versed in living independently and making up our own minds, but that doesn't make us power-crazy nutters. That doesn't mean we need to hold the reins all the time (although maybe some of it). Relaxing and having someone else look after you can be damn good fun.

Women might do a lot of things better than men, but that doesn't mean we can't choose to take the back seat sometimes. It's like the fact that we like to wear girlie skirts and cook sometimes – not because we belong in the kitchen or because we're genetically programmed to wear dresses, but because it gives us an opportunity to enjoy being feminine. Femininity is gorgeous, sexy and fun! And, unfortunately, it so often gets neglected nowadays. But the last place to neglect it is on a first date.

Yet men have been programmed into not being forceful and forthright in their actions and their romantic gestures. Poor things! But chivalry shouldn't be allowed to die. Think Sir Lancelot. Think Richard Gere in *Pretty Woman*. Think Harrison Ford in *Sabrina*. Think Mr Darcy in *Pride and Prejudice*. Why were they sexy? Because they were chivalrous gentlemen. I love 'em.

But it seems the knight's shining armour is going a little rusty. In a time of supposed Girl Power, men are reluctant to don the black poloneck of chivalry and absail down the towering cliff-face of love to proclaim their good intentions. The soft-centre of the so-called New Man is more likely to melt in your hand than to melt a woman's heart. Men are expected to have wash-board stomachs and also be a dab-hand with the ironing-board, to sizzle at bedtime but also at the cooker, to be a Real Man but not too much of a Real Man – and to be romantic but not to be clichéd. It's all rather a lot to live up to, so give him some help! And all you men out there, start polishing your armour!

Do it to me One More Time

OR

Sex

There are just two words to say about sex:

The first is **yes**.

And the second is **please**.

I like to think that, being half-English and half-French, I have an unusual perspective on sex. My French-half revels in its delights. In France, people pop into sex shops in the same way that the English pop out to get a pint of milk. 'I'm just nipping down the sex shop,' they shout to their families and housemates. 'Anybody want anything?'

And struggling against that is my English-half. English people don't like to talk about sex. They don't like doing it, so the story goes, and they certainly don't enjoy it. That would be obscene. The Brits may have a stiff upper lip, but it seems that that's all they have.

One thing's for sure: I only learned the word moderation about seven years ago. It was one in the eye – not literally, you understand – so I slowed my sex life down to a speed at which I could actually enjoy it. It was then that, while I knew that you could happily go at it morning, noon and night and that it shouldn't ever be locked up and hidden away, I realised that there was one nugget of truth I'd missed under the duvet:

SEX DOES NOT EQUAL LIFE

Sex is nothing to be ashamed of, and sex with the right person is the best way *I* can think of to while away a rainy Sunday afternoon, but it's nothing to scream and shout about either. At least not without understanding neighbours. The trick is to be at ease with it. Just relax and enjoy it. It is what it is: neither French nor English – but somewhere in the middle. No, down a bit. Left a bit. Yes. Just there. Wonderful.

BODY TALK

Face it – having sex involves getting naked. That's the fun of it. And if you're not comfortable in your birthday suit, then you're probably not comfortable with sex. And that is not sexy.

When I was in my teens I was a Battersea Dog's Home of puppy fat. I looked in the mirror and saw a blob. And blobs, I worried, were not sexy. You may have heard of the following:

- ♥ **sex symbols**
- ♥ **sex studs**
- ♥ **sex gods and goddesses**
- ♥ **sex muffins**

But have you heard of a **sex blob**? Exactly.

But look at Marilyn Monroe, Sophie Dahl, Kate Winslet. None of them are super-svelte athletic types – although OK they're not blobs – and they're all irresistible to the opposite sex. The things is, sexiness isn't so much to do with the shape you are as how you feel about the shape you are. In short, stand up and stand proud. Especially the men.

Besides, anyone can have a body like a supermodel. All it needs is the bizarre inclination to:

♥ spend all day in the gym, pumping iron

♥ pop vitamins like Smarties

♥ only eat lettuce

♥ get at least 12 hours sleep each night

♥ spend at least 8 hours a day on a regime of beauty treatments

It's just that most of us have lives. But with super-beings popping out of the newspapers and magazines, leaping off the catwalk into our living-rooms day after day, it's no wonder that Joe and Josephine Public are experiencing a bit of an image problem. In short, they don't know whether they're coming or going. Actually, they just know that they're not coming.

The truth is that sexiness is all about oozing happiness and confidence, regardless of what you look like. That's the first lesson. REMEMBER IT!

YOU MAY BEGIN

There are two stages in a new relationship:

- ♥ getting-to-know-each-other
- ♥ getting-to-know-each-other-very-well-indeed

The timing of that momentous moment when your relationship moves from one to the other is sometimes out of your hands. They'll be busy elsewhere. But once that first kiss happens, you can be sure that sex isn't far behind. You've crossed that invisible boundary that marks the divide between friend and official love interest. Now it's only a matter of time. Ultimately, when and how a couple get down to it is a matter for the two adults concerned to decide. It should be a grown-up mutual decision, like buying curtains – though that comes much later and will be greeted less enthusiastically by the man.

One-night stands, of course, are a different matter entirely. They're not for me – as you'll have gathered by now I'm most definitely a romantic and Love is what I'm after – but if that's what you're up for that's fine. Just remember that the two stages are necessarily somewhat compressed when you've only got twelve hours to fit in getting-to-know-each-other, getting-to-know-each-other-very-well-indeed, a quick but uncomfortable coffee and a rapid exit . . .

But we're talking about Happily Ever After in this book, and in my experience it's rare that a one-night stand leads to eternal happiness. And any relationship that starts with sex is bound to be tricky because:

LUST, NOT LOVE, IS BLIND

Lust gets in the way of getting to know each other as people – all you can see is a sex object. There's this niggling feeling you're supposed to be discovering his personality but all you can focus on is his penis. It's distracting. So if you're aiming for a long-term relationship, try and wait at least two weeks after that first kiss before you jump into bed. And, in an ideal world (but we're talking *very* ideal here), try to hold on for two months between first hello and first shag. This might sound impossible, but I've done it without the aid of superhuman powers and – as well as getting you thoroughly overexcited – it does have one key benefit: it allows you to plan for your first time. This isn't simply a question of getting your flat-mates out of the way, but an opportunity to make the first time something really special – to make a really big thing of it. Quite possibly in more senses than one.

The perfect evening

Firstly, begin with the understanding that if you feel it's all a big mistake *in flagrante* (that's the Italian Stallion's way of saying 'in the middle of doing it'), you will stop. Nobody is under any obligation here and it's never too late to back out. Or to get him to.

Secondly, make sure you're not in a car. Cars are fine for quickies, providing you don't mind being jammed up against the gear-stick and having one leg stuck through the sun-roof, but they aren't really appropriate for a leisurely exploration of each other's bodies. They have some pretty major disadvantages:

♥ the seats are never big enough

♥ the steamy windows attract unwanted attention

♥ the suspension gets done in

♥ you end up setting off the air-bags

♥ it's impossible to get it out of the upholstery

♥ you'll have to wear L-plates to protect your modesty

Even the plushest of cars are not romantic, you just end up with more expensive bruises and a larger cleaning bill. So save the auto-erotica for later in your relationship. For now you want a long, protracted evening.

Other places not to have sex for the first time include:

♥ Anywhere near your parents. This is not conducive to a relaxed, erotic experience

♥ Outdoors. You can do the kinky outdoors stuff later, but getting caught in the act won't help your first time to go with a bang

♥ Any form of transport – cars, planes etc. All forms of transport combine the problems of cars with the problems of the outdoors. Not good.

♥ Somewhere you can hear your friends chatting. Not only will you feel inhibited, but there's a danger you'll get distracted by their conversation ('Gosh, I didn't know Emma fancied Mick. I wonder how long that's been going on ... Oh sorry, darling, of course I'm enjoying myself. Hmm. Lovely.')

♥ A waterbed. It's just too difficult to go with the flow. You'll end up in peals of giggles.

If we're talking the ideal world, then for your first time together you'd go away for the weekend to a romantic castle with lots of turrets and white horses. Or a nice country hotel. Of course this does mean that the pressure's on – you both know what the weekend is for. It's a dirty weekend, for God's sake! But whenever you get down to it there's going to be pressure. So you might as well have pressure in pleasant surroundings.

Failing that, try lighting some candles. Candlelight is a good, kind, flattering light that isn't so dark you're left fumbling around, grabbing bits you didn't mean to grab, thinking you're on to a winner only to find you've been holding the bed-post for five minutes, moving in for a long, slow kiss only to find you're about to suck her big toe. But nor is it so bright that you feel like you're on the set of *Emmanuelle,* all your bumps and blemishes lit up in full Technicolor detail with surround-sound and Dolby stereo.

My best tip is for the girl to disappear to the bathroom and return in a flattering sarong. The sarong is a miracle garment when it comes to sex. This simple piece of fabric:

♥ does away with bra-strap fiddling – bras are impossible to remove with anything approaching grace

♥ is extremely flattering. It eliminates that panic that you haven't been to the gym since you paid a small fortune for membership six months ago

♥ is useful to slip into after the event, thus eliminating the body-conscious embarrassment you might feel early on in the relationship – that golden era before you start blithely wandering around stark naked, lazily scratching your private parts with little concern for the picture you're presenting to the world.

♥ This really shouldn't need pointing out but just in case you're wondering – a man who returns from the bathroom in a sarong will not get quite the same response. Not even if he's David Beckham. Oh all right, MAYBE if he's David Beckham.

Other preparation includes the following. The more kinky among you might have your own personal requirements, but you'd best keep those to yourself. For the rest of us I recommend:

♥ make sure you know where the bathroom is, so that you can return to it later to adjust your hair, reapply or remove your smudged Kiss-style mascara, tone down any man-rash etc.

♥ have a box of tissues and a glass of water to hand (the necessity for these should be self-explanatory – and if it's not, then I apologise, but I'm not in the mood to be sufficiently graphic to explain).

♥ make sure suitable contraception is readily available – i.e. by the bed, with the cellophane taken off the box (it's impossible to remove in less than two hours by candlelight).

♥ have the remote controls for both stereo and TV close to hand. When all is done, you don't want to have to move.

When all is in place, you may begin.

LOSING YOUR L-PLATES

Sex can be scary. Particularly if it's your first time with someone. I'm not going to get into the whole losing-your-virginity thing here but suffice to say that's *really* scary, and should be approached with both caution and a clear head. But even if you're a seasoned shagger, sex in the early days of a new relationship can be both intense and nerve-wracking. If you've followed my advice and got to know each other before getting physical then having subconsciously teased each other for weeks, you'll both be absolutely gagging for it.

The thing to remember is that a build-up like this might also build up unrealistic expectations that your first attempt will be a slow and sensuous, fast and furious, perfectly timed and expertly choreographed affair that would make any Hollywood effort look positively amateurish. **It won't.** The first time will not be shot in soft focus. It will be a gritty, messy, clumsy and far from balletic event. The meeting of two new bodies couldn't be anything less.

Three things to forget exist:

- ♥ grace
- ♥ poise
- ♥ elegance

Good sex between two people is learned and practised, the result of getting to know each other mentally and physically. Good sex between *more* than two people needs choreography, but that's another brown-paper-wrapped-book altogether.

It's a good idea to talk about sex before you actually get

down to it – but not right before it, of course, as that might seem a little clinical and will certainly kill any spontaneity. There's no need to go into the gory details, but talking sex not only sets the ground rules, but makes for some great foreplay – or fore-foreplay, as it were. It might become too unbearable to finish the conversation, but try and see it through to the last sentence.

And one last thing for the girls: if, when you're not yet ready for sex, a man says 'Let's go upstairs, I just want to cuddle,' he's lying. He's operating against all the laws of nature. He is probably the devil.

LET'S GET PHYSICAL

Now don't think you're going to get an in-depth account of what I like in bed. Or a step-by-step guide to multiple orgasms. If that's what you're after, you can trot down to your local bookshop and buy a copy of *The Joy Of Sex*. This book is about dating, not shagging, but I do – of course – have a few tips for you.

Getting relaxed
You've got your candlelight, your sarong and your mood music so what you need now is contact. If it's been two weeks since your first kiss then chances are you'll be ripping each other's clothes off, but if you're not the clothes-ripping type, and need to be eased into the situation, massage is the way forward. Make sure you've got some nice-smelling massage oil – not too girly, not too masculine – and get hot and sticky. One small point though, don't let the massage go on for too long or you may not get the reaction you were hoping for.

My friend Ellen decided that the first time she and her new boyfriend, Matt, made love it was going to be perfect. So she invited him round for an intimate dinner for two (having packed her flatmate off to a mate's for the night) and made sure it was the most romantic experience possible. Candles, flowers, champagne and a delicious meal full of exquisite taste sensations that just left you desperate for more (and didn't cause sticky-out stomach syndrome). After a fantastic meal, they retired to the bedroom where she lit more candles, put on some mood music and returned in a sarong (clever girl). She'd earlier made sure there was some musk-scented massage oil by the bed, and offered to do the honours. As he stripped naked in front of her and lay face-down on the bed, you could have cut the sexual tension in the room with a knife. She straddled his lovely pert bottom, got the oil out and started massaging. Now Ellen's very good with her hands, and soon he was moaning in a mixture of ecstasy and excitement. She had him where she wanted him. But, keen to prolong the suspense, she kept going a little longer. He went quiet and, assuming he was just feeling uncontrollably turned on and biting his lip, she carried on. It was only when he started snoring that she realised she'd gone a bit too far. Poor Ellen. (Although I should point out that they did have mind-blowing sex the next morning.)

So a massage can be a hugely erotic experience, but you've got to tread a fine line between relaxing your lover so much they fall asleep on you, and prolonging the massage so that your lover is so totally aroused that he or she is ready to kiss every inch of your body in gratitude.

Of course kissing every inch of your lover's body is also a good way to get going.

Gymnastics

A lot of people obsess about sexual positions – how many, how contorted, how athletic. I hate to break this to those of you who've been aiming for Olympic gold, but sex isn't a competition. Inventive, exciting positions can be a very good thing – certain positions can make the earth move – but trying to get your leg round his head with his arm behind your back and your big toe up his bottom is more like hard work than an erotic experience. If that's what you're after, play twister. It makes less mess and you can tell your parents about it afterwards.

My friend Emily actually managed to pull a muscle recently, so athletic were she and Greg getting in the sack. As far as I gather (although she was understandably a bit reticent about the whole thing) they were trying some sort of winding legs round necks position and when she suddenly got cramp it was virtually impossible to extricate themselves. She was left with a distinct limp for a week. You've been warned!

Open Wide!

OK, we had to get to oral sex at some point, and here's the thing. Oral sex has to be two-way. It's no good lying there while your lover does delicious things to you and then refusing to return the favour. That's cheating. But you've got to seem enthusiastic about it. That's half the turn-on. Someone half-heartedly messing around with your naughty bits is never going to be fun.

Two tips

♥ My friend Jenny (her again) swears by mouthwash. Apparently a good long rinse with some strong mouthwash gets things tingling like never before. And apparently this is a trick that works for both men and women. But I wouldn't guarantee that your teeth will feel clean afterwards.

♥ I've heard – from quite a dubious source – that humming while giving head has remarkable results . I can sort of see the logic, but the thought of humming onto someone's willy just makes me want to giggle. And that's probably not the effect you're looking for. But if it works for you, let me know. If I can keep a straight face for long enough, I might just try it.

Wrong hole

I'm really not going to get into this. All I have to say is, if you must get into this then keep clean! You don't know what's been there. Or rather you do, and that's what worries me.

And guys – don't think we don't know what you're trying to do when you say 'Oops sorry, I slipped'.

Synchronise your watches

I'd like to point out that while size isn't everything, neither is duration. Some men (the younger ones, generally) seem to think that good sex is just a question of keeping going for as long as possible.

A girlfriend of mine, Suzanne, recently found herself dating a toyboy (he was eighteen, a good decade younger than her). It took a while for them to get to bed but when they decided to go away for a dirty weekend it was clearly going to happen. I've never seen Suzanne so excited, and the thing she was most excited about was the prospect of him being able to keep going for hours. Well, he could certainly keep going for hours. Four hours, in fact. Four hours in the missionary position. Four hours of rhythmic, unchanging thrusting. Suzanne nearly fell asleep. The plus was that she managed to mentally reorganise her office quite effectively, but it wasn't exactly the mind-blowing sexual experience she'd been hoping for. The weekend away ended early.

So, guys, remember that it's not just a question of keeping going. While a two-minute shag is something of a disappointment, four hours – unless you're very inventive – is pushing it. And you run the risk of friction burns.

Food Sex
Now here's a popular one. And it's largely because it combines two of mankind's favourite pastimes – eating and sex. Perfect! But it matters what food you choose:

♥ ICE-CREAM is sexy – cold, creamy, luxurious and delicious

- ♥ PASTA is not – it's just lumpy

- ♥ ASPARAGUS is sexy – especially when it's dripping in butter. (But it will make your pee smell!)

- ♥ CHILLI is not – you could end up with burns in some painful places

- ♥ STRAWBERRIES are sexy – all sweet and juicy as you bite into them

- ♥ CUCUMBERS are not – they're just comic

> My friend Vivien swears by chocolate fondues. What you need is very bitter, rich chocolate melted with butter and cream, and lots of delicious – and suggestive – things to dip in it. Marshmallows are great as the insides melt in the heat of the chocolate, feeding each other strawberries is definitely a good one, and of course dipping a whole banana in the chocolate and licking it off needs little explanation – although I don't suggest that men try this one unless they have very understanding girlfriends with a good sense of humour. One minor warning though: very hot chocolate and naked skin is a dangerous combination. Be careful!

Talking dirty

Personally, I reckon you've got to know someone quite well before you get involved in sexy talk, as otherwise you run the risk of feeling a bit silly, but talking dirty can make what goes on under the duvet very interesting indeed. It's only really by talking about what you both like that you'll find out what you both like, and that's the yellow-brick-road to great sex.

The first thing, however, is that you need to agree on some terms for your naughty bits. Don't ask why but I quite like zizzi, toy-shop or nunney for my bits, and Tommy Todger or plain old willy for his. Well, at least they always raise a smile. If nothing else. But the terms you choose are entirely up to you – although I wouldn't go broadcasting them unless you want all your friends to take the piss mercilessly. Once you've got your lingo sorted, there's nothing left but to get into bed and get chatting.

The only problem with talking dirty is that you have to have a very similar sense of what's sexy and what's just funny. Or off-putting. For example, you wouldn't catch me dead saying:

♥ Do it to me, baby

♥ Impale me on your big love prong OR

♥ Yes, yes, stick it up me, please

But that's just me. I imagine there *are* people who find 'do it to me, baby' hugely sexy – I know some of Jenny's City boys do – so it's just a personal thing.

Actually, Jenny had rather a bad experience recently with a City boy who took talking dirty just a bit too far. He obviously fancied himself as a real love-god, and once they got back to his (black and chrome) flat and into his (silk-sheeted) bed and got down to it, he started shouting things like 'Yes, yes! You love it! It's so

> big! All hot and wet!' Needless to say, Jenny couldn't restrain her giggles and had to leave rather prematurely.

But if you stick to what you're both comfortable with, talking dirty will allow you to get to know each other's peculiarities so that next time it gets that bit better. And the time after that it's better still. And so on until you're exhausted/have to eat/have to go to work etc.

APRÈS-SHAG

There are differing opinions as to what you should both do after the event. Women tend to think – and naturally I agree – that the best thing is to cuddle up. It's important to retain that intimacy, and nothing does this better than simply being close and quiet together.

But a girl who wants to cuddle up is going to have to let her man wander around for a bit first. I know that sounds strange, but after sex, men need their space. They need to take stock of the situation, zone out for a few minutes, deal with their primeval urge to have sex with the next and nearest available cavewoman. Don't be offended. Certain urges need to be dealt with. And the female urge to regress to babytalk and crawl into her man's arms will just have to wait a few minutes.

Remember that, according to Taoist beliefs, the female orgasm is empowering, a life-affirming delivery of new energy. However, an orgasm leaves men utterly shagged. That's why sportsmen are discouraged from having sex the night before a competition. No big events before the big event, as it were. Your man knows that complete après-shag collapse is frowned on by women, and he knows that post-play is as important as foreplay. But he's sorry, he just can't help it. If he's just had sex, he can't stay still *and* awake. So the need for space and the need for sleep will manifest themselves in a number of ways:

- ♥ walking around the room looking for pants and socks

- ♥ talking about something of no relevance to the situation at all

- ♥ falling so soundly asleep you'll think he's concussed

- ♥ turning on the TV, the radio – anything but you

If he rolls over and fall asleep (the classic manoeuvre) don't let this upset you too much. You might even take it as a compliment – he's comfortable enough in your presence to fall asleep. You'd take it as a compliment if your passenger nodded off while you were driving, wouldn't you? In short, if men just can't help acting on impulse, then neither can they help sleeping on orgasm. It's like the irritating way that photocopiers automatically switch themselves off because they're suddenly short of toner.

Alternatively, he may switch on the TV without so much as a hushed expression of life-long commitment. If the football is on, you may be a little alarmed that he suddenly finds the animation he was lacking only seconds before. But if it's a film, or something you can enjoy together – and, should the chance for a second run come along, ignore together – then be content. Let him have his space for while. Then take it away from him. In the meantime:

Congratulations, you've just had a wonderful time.

So, boys, I've just apologised for you. Explained your irritating behaviour. I hope you're grateful. And here's what you've got to do for me in return. Just try to stay awake, and in bed, with the TV off, for five minutes. It might not be as bad as you think. Start at one minute and work your way up to five. Or, if you can't manage even one minute, just say something nice to the lovely girl you've just had the most fabulous time with. Please. It will make her day.

TOP DOG

Relationships have rules – unspoken ones, unacknowledged ones, subconscious ones. They help you to know where you stand. These rules do not, however, help you to know where you lie down. There are no rules in the bedroom. Or the car or on the kitchen table – wherever passion grabs you.

This means that, although you may relate to each other in a particular way outside the bedroom – your relationship may be one of equality, shared tasks, roles that you're both happy with – this has no bearing on what goes on once you're testing the springs. Although making love should, of course, be grounded in balance and harmony, it's quite possible that on the surface at least, one of you will be Top Cat.

And yes, it's usually the man. This tends to suit men, because of the Alpha Male instinct. It could be that they are not in control in any other area of their life, but here is their chance to be masterful. The Alpha Male becomes the Alpha Mate. And in my experience most women, no matter how high-powered, career-driven or masterful they may be when they're in a suit, simply want a big strong man when they're naked.

Of course it might well work the other way round – the woman may assert herself much more strongly in the bedroom – whatever works for your both. But don't be alarmed just because your day-to-day relationship takes a different turn under the duvet. This is fine and dandy.

Although you should perhaps be slightly worried when one of you produces a lead and asks the other to roll over.

A FEW HITCHES

Never mind public speaking, first time sex is *really* terrifying. There are so many opportunities for nerves to spoil the fun. So much can be so wrong – too quick, too slow, too cack-handed. While your libido is doing somersaults, your stomach is completing a trans-Atlantic crossing. In a barrel.

Women are naturally going through the standard 'but I don't look like Pamela Anderson' paranoia, but men too have their worries. In particular, performance anxiety. Most men are, now more than ever, body-conscious – although they're still more likely worry about what a state it's in than to do anything about it. And as well as coping with the endless male models with a xylophone for a stomach and nutcracker thighs on fitness magazines and billboards, men have to worry about the size of their appendage. Is it big enough? Is it long enough? And he's heard somewhere that it's actually *circumference* that matters so is it wide enough? Does she have strong feelings on circumcision? Guys, you've got what you've got and – short of some pretty bizarre and unpleasant surgery – there's nothing you can do to change it so be proud of your penis and I'm sure we'll be just delighted with it.

On top of this he'll be concerned about getting it up – and he'll be ready with a long list of excuses (nerves, alcohol, stress, too many Polos) just in case his equipment doesn't pass its MOT – and there's also that terrible fear of a woman wondering whether that's as far up as it gets when it's as far up as it gets.

Whether he goes the distance is also a potential problem – while women's genitals require fine-tuning to get a good reception, men's are volatile chemicals, ready to explode at the slightest movement. And they're even more unpredictable with a strange body. In fact **Davina's Unfortunate Law of Orgasms** is to blame for a lot of frustration:

The male rule of orgasms:

♥ the **less** he knows the woman's body, the **more** likely he is to orgasm.

The female rule of orgasms:

♥ the **more** a man knows her body, the **more** likely she is to orgasm.

Just Mother Nature's little joke, I guess.

Men will also worry about their technique. And the problem is that while he'll probably want you to know what you're doing, he'll also want everything he does to be a completely new experience for you – and chances are it won't be. If you really get honest with the details pre-sex, remember that men always tend to over-estimate the number of partners they've had, and women, wisely, tend to underestimate. The idea is, I suppose, that women should simply know their trade but be subtle about it. Anyway, don't knock it. It's a mutually-agreed fallacy that tends to work.

One last thing: try not to make sex 'an issue'. Talking too much about sex – unless it's that special kind of talking about sex – can be like putting a damp towel over a flame. Over-analysis just creates pressure. Sex becomes a topic of conversation rather than something to simply do and enjoy. If your partner's not in the mood, try and get them in the mood. But don't be offended if they're not. A lot can easily get in the way of the libido, even with a new partner.

THE BIG OOOHHHHH!

One important message here:

DON'T FAKE IT!

Faking orgasms, as well as being dishonest, doesn't bode well for the long-term future of your relationship. Most women have done it. All my friends have at some point, because it gets the whole thing over with. But don't do it in a long-term relationship.

Men, of course, don't generally have too much trouble reaching orgasm – some might say they have too little trouble. But women have to take their time. Everything has to be in place and there's no point in forcing it. Above all, remember that it's not a holy grail. Women shouldn't think they're flattering the man by pretending and men shouldn't hassle the woman to orgasm – that's a sure-fire way to make sure it doesn't happen. There are plenty of women who have never had an orgasm – far more than you might imagine – so men need to take care with what may well be a delicate subject, and women need to be open about it.

And men shouldn't respond by making it a personal quest to provide the first. It's not a competition. There are no prizes and no cash equivalent. Sometimes it happens. Sometimes it doesn't. Neither of you should throw a strop if it doesn't. Just take your time and try again later. Trying is half the fun of sex, after all.

> I used to know a bloke called Chris who – I was reliable informed by his best friend – took pride in bringing every woman he ever slept with to orgasm. His best friend told me this extraordinary fact, and expected me to burst into rapturous praise for Chris's sensitivity and sexual prowess. But I was absolutely horrified! I can't imagine anything worse than someone trying to force a girl to orgasm. It must be a nightmare. I had visions of some poor female tied to a bed for days on end while Chris beavered away, desperately trying to make her bells ring. Ugh. Horrible.

SURPRISE!

One thing you might like to discuss before the big occasion is any little surprises you have lying in wait for your would-be lover. Tattoos, Bobbit-type scars, birthmarks, piercings – especially those in the nether regions – might shock, so a tip-off is a good idea.

But if your lover has a surprise in store, be open-minded! You might not like her tattoo to start with, but if you love her you'll grow to love the tattoo too – assuming it's not a ex-boyfriend's name, or a tally of lovers. Similarly, if you love someone, be willing to make changes to your bodily adornment if it's traumatising your beloved – this isn't so easy with tattoos of course (a large plaster might help), but piercings might be removed. I took out my nipple piercing, for instance – largely because nobody knew what to do with it, myself included. It just sat there, worrying people.

Communicating is also important as it's a long, hard process to try and guess what each of you likes and doesn't like. It's so much simpler to actually say what you do and don't find sexy. And it can also save you a lot of time. Discovering, for example, that the only way your new partner can enjoy sex is wearing a pair of stockings over his head and with a piece of orange peel in his mouth, or that whipping is absolutely essential, could take a while. And you may be trysexual – prepared to try anything once – but sexual compatibility is important to any long-term relationship. Could you face forty years of the cat-o-nine-tails?

Clearly someone with a predilection for pornography is not going to get it on with someone who considers it a blight on society. Of course, freedom of choice is important – if that's what somebody is into, then as long as nobody is hurt (against their will, that is), then that's their choice. But so is the freedom to say 'no thank-you very much'. And generally speaking, if you wait a while before jumping into bed together, you'll get a sense of what your new bedfellow-to-be's sexual tastes are. There's always the odd dark horse who turns up in the pantomime donkey outfit, but they're rare. Don't be pressured into joining them if that's not your bag, but if you like the idea, make sure you swap ends occasionally.

Finally, I'm unconvinced about the advice of a hundred sex manuals that you should get to know your own body intimately – the prospect of poking around with a carefully angled mirror is not something that's ever really grabbed me – but you should be prepared to let your partner explore the details. It often happens that a lover knows your body better than you do yourself. And this is great – sex is a very special gift from one person to another. They should be allowed to unwrap it.

IT'S ALL IN THE DETAILS

A sign of a good relationship, of love really, is not the quality or quantity of sex but your partner's attitude to your hang-ups. A boyfriend who tells a woman that she should start going to the gym or needs to diet shouldn't be put up with.

He should be shown the DOOR.

It's the making of a confidence crisis. The same goes for any woman who tells her man that his pecs aren't big enough and he needs to lift something heavier than the remote control occasionally. Love should not be conditional on looks. A person should love you for who you are and the way you are. And certainly not for the blonde, big-busted bombshell he thinks you might become with a nip and tuck, a lettuce leaf and some peroxide. He's simply got the wrong woman. He will probably never have the right one.

When I meet someone and start to explore those intimate little body bits, I tend to react in one particular way: I lose weight because I'm super-excited all the time. And then, when the relationship has a solid foundation, I start to put the weight back on.

And then some.

My grandmother always said that cooking is the way to a man's heart. Of course, cooking certain things all the time is the way to stop it too. But there is some innate connection between healthy, plentiful eating and the first throes of a real love. It's like a mutual acceptance that body shape doesn't really matter. Pass the chips.

So what you eat shouldn't affect your sex life (unless of course you're eating it off each other). PMT, however, affects your sex life a great deal, as women's attitude to sex tends to depend on their monthly cycle. My self-confidence changes as the month progresses: when ovulating, and just before, I feel sexiest (obviously a biological drive to have sex when most fertile). Also, oddly enough, just before my period I feel jolly frisky.

But about a week before my period, for a couple of days I'm most definitely NOT:

♥ sexy

♥ vivacious

♥ fun to be around

♥ considerate

♥ loving

Instead I AM:

♥ weepy

- ♥ angry

- ♥ frustrated

- ♥ fragile

- ♥ needy

Oh yes, and a bit of a lump who needs a hug but who terrorises anyone who dares come anywhere near me. Sex is, at this point, not high on my agenda. So, men, please be a bit understanding. Be patient, and the love of your life will be eternally grateful. But let's look on the bright side:

> **For quite a few days every month,**
> **women are definitely up for it,**
> NO QUESTION.

A BIT OF EXPERIMENTATION

This section is for the adventurous. Some people are happy to stick to the bedroom, and the missionary position, but not everybody. We're all increasingly experimenting, so here are a few ideas to spice things up. (But let me just state that I haven't necessarily tried them all.)

Places and spaces I've been

The most obvious way to bring a bit of excitement into your sex life is to leave the bedroom. You don't have to go far, of course – the shower is always an exhilarating experience, and we've all heard the stories about washing machines and tumble dryers. Don't think it works with dishwashers though. If you're lucky enough to have a real fire, kick the cats out of the way and do it there. Or just try sneaking up on your lover while they're cooking or washing up, putting your arms round them, moving your hands down, and see what happens.

If you're going to leave the comfort of your own home, the fresh air is quite bracing. Beaches, fields, or just the garden, it's a getting-back-to-nature thing. Which is why doing it in a dirty alleyway behind the pub doesn't have quite the same effect.

> I've got a friend who swears by a particular beach – she made me promise not to tell you which one – which gets absolutely deserted in the evenings. She and her man go down there with a bottle of wine and a couple of glasses, build a fire, lie down, and get all sandy as the sun sets over the sea. Perfect.

One small point though – try not to get caught. A bit of danger can be quite exciting, but the local farmer pointing a large shotgun at you is probably a bit more danger than you need.

Another friend of mine claims to have had sex in a tree, but I'm not sure if I believe him. Even if it's true, it doesn't sound very pleasurable. I just thought you'd like to know . . .

Going indoors again – or sort-of indoors, it's at this stage in a relationship that transport can come into its own. Now I'm not in any way condoning having sex on public transport, IT'S ILLEGAL SO DON'T DO IT, but I've promised to tell you everything I know so here goes. Planes, I gather, aren't as much fun as you'd think. Sure, there's the whole mile-high club thing, but apparently it's all quite uncomfortable. Trains, however, are a completely different matter.

> I have more than one friend who swears by the Bluebell heritage line train – it's got separate carriages, no corridor and there are twenty minutes between stops. Perfect. Of course if the train gets held up – as trains are wont to do – then you can end up having quite an audience, but that – they tell me – is part of the fun.

Beaches, planes and trains are all quite run-of the mill though, so if you want to get into the REALLY STRANGE category I reckon you've got to liven up your venues with a theme. One friend of mine (you've guessed it, Jenny) visits gun clubs for her thrills. Of course she doesn't actually have sex there – you wouldn't really want to break the rules in a place run by people you know to be armed and dangerous – but she drags whoever her latest man is along to a gun club to get them in the mood. Magnums, she says, are very sexy. Firing a gun makes her want to unload his chamber. So there you go.

That one I sort of understand. The next one I don't.

> Carol went out with Philip for just over a year. We all used to sit around talking about sex a lot – and Carol had always been the most vocal – but while she was with Philip she went mysteriously quiet. We all assumed she was just loved-up so had decided to stop sharing the gory details, but after they split up she

revealed that he had a very peculiar fetish indeed: he loved having sex in places he'd studied. When they were dating he was studying at the College of Law (I'm not telling you which one) and he used to cajole her into meeting him at the pub next door after she'd finished work. They'd spend most of the evening in the pub with his mates, and when they left he used to drag her into the College of Law toilets for a shag. Now that was quite strange, but it was when they went to a May ball at his old Oxbridge college (you see, being unspecific again; aren't I discreet!) and after five minutes he dragged her into the loos there, that she decided it was just too weird. We never quite managed to fathom the psychological implications of Philip's strange obsession, but Carol was definitely better off without him.

Doctors and Nurses

Dressing up is another old favourite – of people generally, I mean. Not me specifically. And as long as you're both comfortable with your costumes, then anything goes. French maids, hookers, teacher and pupil, boss and secretary, babies . . . well personally I'd steer clear of men who like to dress up as babies, but if it works for you – and you can keep a straight face – then fine.

The strangest dressing-up story I ever heard, however, involved one of my favourite superheroes.

When my friend Charlie was a student, he had this very strict tutor called Mr Henry. Mr Henry was utterly straight-laced and totally fierce – and not very popular with the students. Mr Henry, however, quite liked Charlie for some reason, so Charlie had been round to Mr Henry's flat a couple of times to collect books or hand essays in late. So one day, when he needed some textbook or other which wasn't in the library, he decided to pop round to Mr Henry's to collect it. He arrived at the door to hear some very peculiar noises from within. It was all a bit muffled, but he could hear a woman (presumably Mr Henry's equally straight-laced wife) screaming. Charlie was naturally rather alarmed, and went to get the downstairs neighbour for help. They couldn't break down the door – and the screaming was getting worse – so, terrified by this point, they called the police. When the police arrived and they all stormed in, they found Mr Henry's wife securely tied to the bed, naked, legs spread, with a gag in her mouth. And there was a loud thumping coming from inside the wardrobe. When they opened it, out fell Mr Henry in a perfect size 18 Batman suit complete with mask and ears. Apparently what had happened was that he'd tied Mrs Henry to the bed, then climbed on top of the wardrobe to jump down – Batman style – and save her. Unfortunately, his weight was a bit much for the wardrobe and he fell through the top into all the clothes. Even more unfortunately, it only unlocked from the outside. I know this sounds like an urban myth, but Charlie was there and he saw it. And Charlie's a trustworthy boy – if a little indiscreet.

There were three in the bed . . .

Threesomes. Group sex. Orgies. A bit dangerous, I'd say.

And not dangerous because of nasty diseases, but because it's a rare person who can watch their beloved getting friendly with someone else's pubic hair and not get just the tiniest bit hot and bothered. And when you're back in a twosome and he/she is doing the same thing to you, you're going to get flashbacks. It's inevitable. And it's horrible.

The other problem with threesomes is that you'll never agree on who the third person should be. Most girls are going to prefer a threesome with two men, and EVERY man is going to want a threesome with two women. And there isn't a compromise – except a foursome, and that's just two couples having sex in the same room. So someone's going to be feeling a bit put out before you even get into bed, and that's not going to help you get relaxed.

All in all, if you're in a serious relationship, keep your sex life one-on-one. If you're bored by having sex with just each other, turn the TV on. (Joke!)

Bondage

Bondage is a little word that covers a wide range of things. We've all tried bondage in some way – everyone experiments with the odd bit of tying up and blindfolding – but you've got to make sure you feel secure with whoever's tying you up. You don't want him to wander off to the pub, starve you to death, get out the camera or invite his friends round for a viewing. But of course the risk is part of the thrill, so you're treading a fine line. So remember to:

♥ Make sure you're tied up with something soft – tights are good but stockings are sexier. You don't want to end up with tell-tale ligature marks engraved into your wrists for days on end.

♥ Don't tie anything so tight that it cuts off the circulation. Blue hands are not sexy. Also, make sure you or your partner could escape if they really needed to.

♥ Don't use this opportunity to torment your tied-up partner. If they really hate being tickled, don't do it. This is also not the time to tell them what's going wrong in the relationship. Just because they're helpless doesn't mean you should take advantage of them. Or only sexually.

If you're going the whole way and doing the blindfold thing as well, make the most of the fact that your partner can't see what you're doing and surprise them.

♥ Ice cubes

♥ Feathers AND

♥ Hair

can turn good sex into great sex.

Bring on the Gimp

Whips, chains and rubber masks are a different ball-game entirely. Fetishism is getting into the seriously kinky. Which is fine if that's your bag, but be careful if it's not. S&M is a hardcore scene, so if you don't feel ready for it you probably aren't. Of course a bit of rubber is very useful for sucking in those problem areas and giving you Pamela Anderson-style breasts, but personally, people with wardrobes full of rubber bodices and PVC crotchless knickers give me the giggles. Sorry.

Bestiality and Necrophilia

Don't go there. Ever.

Of course there's loads more kinky stuff you could get into, but after all this rubber I'm starting to feel a bit queasy so I think we'll move on now.

A FEW DON'TS

A few final tips on what to **avoid.**

The Office Shag

It's what you've been fantasising about – as far as I can gather it's what everyone's been fantasising about – but if you must do it, BE CAREFUL.

Someone I know (but unfortunately can't name) works in a small company where everyone knows each other – rather intimately, in his case. And after one particularly raucous office party, Robert (the senior marketing executive) and Alison (his secretary) started getting very friendly. They chatted for ages, lips only a tantalisingly few inches apart, and then realised that they were getting some funny looks so decided to slip quietly away to somewhere a bit more private. They took the lift up to the third floor, and made a dash for the boardroom where they stripped naked and had wild passionate sex on the table. The next morning, Robert was at the weekly divisional meeting in that same boardroom – and remembering his rather impressive performance on it the night before – when he realised that the managing director was glaring at him rather hard. After the meeting, the MD took him to one side and explained that the previous night's CCTV had recorded some rather unusual activity in the boardroom. I probably don't need to tell you that Robert didn't last much longer in that job.

Even more bizarre is a story I heard about a bloke and his girlfriend who worked at the same company and got caught shagging in the post room. Twice. How does anyone get caught *twice*? It's beyond me.

Austin Powers

Now I know you weren't expecting a film section in this book, but a quick warning:

Austin Powers can ruin your sex life.

I was having lunch with my mate Beatrice the other day and it was clear that she had something to tell me. She alternated between looking as if she was about to spill the beans, seeming very upset, and giggling to herself. I finally got her talking, and it turned out that her boyfriend, Theo, had come home the previous night with a video of the first Austin Powers film – which he knew she really wanted to see. She was over the moon and they settled down on the sofa. However, although it's a fantastic film, they somehow got a bit distracted and before you could say 'shagadelic', they were making love on the floor. But just as Beatrice was really enjoying herself, Theo let out a snort of laughter and she realised that he was still watching the film. She was livid! It's a very funny film, but don't try to have sex while it's on.

Getting caught

Getting caught in the act is a very bad thing. And particularly bad if it's a family member who catches you.

My mate Diana is particularly obsessive about maximum privacy when it comes to shagging after being caught by her grandmother. She and her boyfriend had got a bit carried away – thinking her grandmother was out – up in Diana's bedroom. It was one of those quick emergency shags, and they'd got carried away so quickly that they were both still fully clothed – if a bit rearranged – when her grandmother came into the room. Fortunately they both looked decent, so Granny just looked a bit surprised that Diana was sitting on her boyfriend's lap. And that she didn't move. Diana's long dress covered all the embarrassing bits, so she and her boyfriend just sat there – Tommy Tucker still inside the toy-shop – and had a strange, politely stilted conversation about what to have for dinner before her Grandmother left. No wonder she's got a lock on her bedroom door nowadays.

I really felt for Diana when she told me about this embarrassing experience, but it absolutely paled into oblivion when I heard about Amy's nightmare shag.

> When my friend Amy was about eighteen, she and her boyfriend Ben went out on a Saturday night with their mates and got particularly hammered. Now I'm not just talking quite pissed and having a good time – we're into serious memory loss territory here. Anyway, they got back to her house (where she lived with her parents) at about three in the morning, feeling distinctly horny. Going up to her room didn't seem to be an option – partly because it was too close to her parents' bedroom and partly because they were tearing each other's clothes off the minute they got in the door – so they got down to it on the sitting-room floor. The only problem is that they were so drunk that they didn't get very far before they both passed out cold. They did, however, get far enough that when her parents came downstairs the next morning they were a little surprised to find Amy and Ben, stark naked, rather graphically entangled on the floor. I won't go into detail about the fact that the condom appeared to have disappeared up inside Amy, as it might put you off your food.

But that does lead me on rather effectively to the next section.

WHAT TO WEAR – A VERY SERIOUS BIT

Now I hate to get heavy – I don't want to sound like your mother – but we've got to talk about contraception. More particularly, you and your partner have got to talk about contraception, rather than fumbling around in the heat of the moment or, worse still, not bothering in the heat of the moment. We all know about AIDS, so get used to the idea: condoms are essential. Without a diving suit, you don't get in the water. Simple as that.

Can you name the last ten people your partner had sex with? And the last ten people each of them had sex with? If the answer is yes than you either have an extremely thick address book and an extensive network of particularly close friends, or you're kidding yourself. Faced with a blossoming romance your instinct might be to trust your gorgeous new lover, but this is one moment to be cold and considered.

Ironically, lots of couples tend to start off using condoms and then, after time, dispense with them, as though trust leads to some mystical clearing up of sexual diseases. It doesn't. And AIDS and the like hits nice, ordinary people – not just groupie-infested rockers. So get an AIDS test. You don't have to give your real name, it won't affect your life insurance and no one else need know.

And there's another very good reason for contraception: you can't enjoy sex if you're worrying all the time, either about disease or unwanted pregnancy. If you can't enjoy it, what's the point.

NO SHOWER, NO SHAGGING

My final point
Preparation for sex should include plenty of scrubbing – of each other if that's the way you want it, though most people save that for after they've made love. You should be spotless

in every nook and corner. Nothing is more of a turn-off than unpleasant whiffs in the knicker department. Hygiene has to be to the max.

Women, I'm told, give off different aromas depending on what they've eaten – something which doesn't bear thinking about too closely. Suffice it to say that bidets are useful for resolving this potentially embarrassing problem (chilli con carne at lunch, perhaps?) as they clean the parts that otherwise only carefully-angled showers can reach. And it's a rather pleasant feeling to get you going anyway.

The bidet, you may well already know, is a French invention. And, as I've said, the French know a lot about sex. The case for cleanliness rests.

My Endless Love

OR

Coupledom

This is where the really hard work begins. And it's what you've been striving for.

Here it is: coupledom.

Coupledom has a bad press amongst the young, free and single, and even those who are coupled-up sometimes look back longingly to their swinging singleton days. Yet, despite the joys of being an independent free spirit, of sowing your cherries and losing your oats – or whatever other euphemism works for you – most of us, deep down, look forward to going to bed with the same person every night. Having someone who knows which buttons you need pressed (no, I'm not talking about the TV remote), sex you can practise till it's perfect. I know I did. Let's enter the wonderful world of coupledom . . .

BACK TO THE SINGLE LIFE

OK, that's not what you expected. But before we go any further there's something we've got to clear up.

When you're in a relationship, it's tempting to think you'd better bloody well keep at it no matter what. You worked so hard, waited so long for Mr Right to come along, and you can't quite come to terms with the idea that he is, in fact, Mr Not-Quite-There, or Mr It-Was-Great-But-Now-I'm-Not-Too-Sure, or plain old Mr Wrong. You've done your time in the singles wilderness. There's loads of singletons out there just gagging to be in a relationship. You can't just throw one away, can you?

And what if you never find another cuddlebunny? If this man or woman was The One – as you were so quick to tell all your mates, remember? – then surely there won't be another. It stands to reason: he or she can't be The One and also one of a number of possible 'ones'.

It all depends on your philosophy. Women tend to believe there is just one perfect man for them, for whom they are destined by Fate. It doesn't matter that you've never stepped outside of your home town, it just so happens that The One For You hung out at the same local as you. Strange that.

Men, on the other hand, think you have to cast your net wider. There are plenty of fish in the sea. Or, in other words, there are hundreds, perhaps thousands of women that they could quite happily spend the rest of their life with. This isn't terribly romantic.

The truth is actually half way between the two.

♥ Guys – you're unlikely to meet hundreds, even dozens of women you could happily spend your life with. So make sure you appreciate one who turns your life rose-tinted.

♥ Girls – get some perspective. People change. You'll

144

change. And if Mr Right figured you were Ms Wrong, then he was probably Mr Asshole.

The key thing to remember is that if you're in a relationship with Mr or Ms Compromise, then Get Out. It won't last, so you might as well quit before you need a solicitor to extricate yourself.

TACKLING THE ASSAULT COURSE

Coupledom isn't about membership of some exclusive club that won't let single people in. Coupledom is about being in a partnership. And that has many great things to offer:

♥ companionship

♥ a shoulder to cry on

♥ an arm to hide under

♥ a body to toy with as you see fit

♥ someone who will make you tea in the morning

The last of these, while always welcome, is the least important. Although it's nice, it's not in itself worth the effort of being in a couple.

That's right – I said EFFORT.

Since when did effort come into the picture? I hear you cry. I thought being in love was all roses and skipping through meadows. I work hard enough as it is. I don't want to have to work at a relationship too.

Well, if that's where you're at, you should probably stay single. But I'll admit that when you meet Mr or Ms Right, it's hard to remember that romance isn't all – well, romance. You get swept up in the hearts and flowers thing. You've yet to realise that a partnership is an assault course:

- ♥ There are boundaries to draw.

- ♥ You have to get to grips with your new lover's petty hates and bizarre likes.

- ♥ you've got to work out who's boss.

Even the most perfect of relationships – Prince and Princess Charming, Superman and Lois, Posh and Beckham – have their bad days. All right maybe Posh and Becks don't but you know what I mean. It ain't all staring into each other's eyes. Sometimes it's wanting to rip them out. Shocking, isn't it?

And here's my big tip. It's blindingly obvious but it's a bit of advice that so many couples ignore:

- ♥ take things slowly

- ♥ communicate without screaming

- ♥ and together you can overcome just about anything

As Yoda should have said: *be it will, if it is meant. If meant to be together, split up you won't. If not right for you, fail the relationship will.* And if it ain't meant to be, don't fight it. If you're fundamentally incompatible you are, as they say, flogging a dead horse. And anyone who's ever flogged a dead horse knows that it's not a pleasant experience. Think Pedigree Chum.

Remember: being single is at worst neutral and at best fantastic fun. If you're in a bad relationship, call it a day. Go out there and find a good one.

CARELESS TALK COSTS WIVES

It's good to talk. At least that's what the ad says. But conversation between two people in a relationship is much more important, and much more delicate, than ringing up a mate for a chin-wag about the football or Madonna's latest frock. If you can't talk to your loved one, dump them now. That's right, I said **now**. Put down this book (well, perhaps read the chapter on the dumping first), then go and tell them it's over. Thank you.

And I'm not talking about the kind of conversation in which two people shout very loudly. Let's get our definitions right: that's an argument. A conversation is a two-way thing that, hopefully, results in some kind of positive resolution.

Such chats are very very important. But there are some places in which an important conversation should not take place. These include, for instance:

♥ A birthday party

♥ At the cinema

♥ At a concert

♥ Underwater

♥ Long-distance

♥ In bed

The last in this important list is the classic. My grandmother, and yours too probably, told me never to go to bed on an argument. And she was right. That way lies the spare room scenario. And that can be very unpleasant when you don't have a spare room. Nothing is worse than trying to sleep when you're both fuming, lying there with your backs to each other.

The best time to have a proper, serious conversation is over dinner at home. Keep it light and intimate, stay calm, listen to each other and think before you put your foot in it. Admit you're wrong if (God forbid!) you are. Oh, and don't try to attribute blame – the plates will be flying and the door slammed before you know it. Don't fly off the handle. Not even if he's holding his knife like a pen.

A LITTLE 'HELP' FROM YOUR FRIENDS

Falling in love is a wonderful, often overwhelming experience. But it throws you into all sorts of confusion and what looks set to be a long-term relationship can really rock the boat of the life you had:

- ♥ You're suddenly constantly busy

- ♥ Your usual routines get interrupted

- ♥ You might give up things you used to enjoy doing

- ♥ Your friends start forgetting your name

- ♥ You get invited to dinner parties, but only together

AND THAT'S JUST THE START

148

It can be an intoxicating experience to just let go and throw yourself in, to completely wrap yourself up in this new person – both literally and figuratively – and shut out the world.

This is what is commonly known as a BIG MISTAKE.

You'd better hope you have understanding friends. They might expect that in the first few months of a relationship, they're history. They do not exist. They might have known you since you were five and shared milk and biscuits at primary school break-time together, but in the early stages of a new relationship, all that means diddly-squat. A good friend understands this. They've been there themselves.

But don't expect understanding and patience a few months down the line. Once people can't say your name without adding *and [insert partner's name here]*, it's time to start paying your friends some attention.

And it's all even more tricky if your friends aren't so keen on your new partner. The casual announcement that 'he's all wrong for you, his jokes aren't funny and he has ugly hair' is going to cause a few problems. One part of you wants to stay true to your friends, but there's a little devil jumping up and down in your skull, desperate to tell your best friend which bridge they can go and jump off.

But remember that although it's nice if your partner gets on with your mates, it's not vital. My friend Mandi loved her husband but hated his puerile mates. Her wonderful man became a football-crazy, leering, fast-food-and-beer-guzzling yob in their presence. It almost drove her to distraction. But over the years she came to feel quite fond of them – because she was under no pressure to like them. There was none of that 'love me, love my dog' approach (though now I think about it, anyone who loved me would have to love my dog, but that's another story).

COME CLEAN

It's no good spending the first few months of your relationship cooking wonderful meals for your partner, massaging them and making them their favourite drink if the second the relationship is in the bag, all that goes out of the window. The sooner they see your dark side, the better. So come clean **at the beginning** with all your personal problems – not your smelly feet (believe me, they'll already know about that), but your hang-ups and your 'personal issues' as they say in American talk-shows.

I, for instance, have a bad habit of having fits of insecurity. I'm fine in front of huge crowds and cameras, but I worry about how to keep hold of the man I love. Strange, huh? My self-esteem fluctuates madly, and supreme confidence can become severe self-doubt in a matter of minutes. Just a strange glance from my beloved – well, a glance that I perceive as strange – can tip the balance. I'm a super-human can-do-anything type one second, and a quivering ball of pathetic fluff the next.

This is not a condition I would wish to spring on anyone after a long period of the super-human side. It would, to say the least, come as a shock. So I have to be up-front about it, explain that it happens, that I can't help it (although I try my best to control it) and any help from them would be appreciated.

Other people have difficulties in being intimate, or other such emotional hiccups. Everyone – yes, that includes you – has some area or other that leaves them a little bewildered, no matter how much clear thinking they do about it. Don't be embarrassed, just admit it.

But by the same token, don't play up to it either. Pushing

for the sympathy vote is very bad form, and you're shooting yourself in the foot. Remember the little boy who cried wolf? You're the little girl who cried 'don't go out tonight, I'm scared to be alone!'.

THE STIGMA OF COUPLEDOM

> *To Bunnikins,*
> *with oodles of love and stuff,*
> *Hunkster xxx*

That, in short, is why being part of a couple, especially a couple in love, carries such a stigma. It's all just a bit naff, a bit twee, a bit gooey. And, above all, it's all a bit personal. We'd rather not know, thank-you. It all hints at details we'd rather not imagine. So, if you're heading for a relationship, prepare to get some stick. I'm sure you've been known to pull a lemon sherbet face at a couple having a smooch-cum-tongue-sandwich in the middle of the street. **Take it away!**

Touchy-feely-gropey couples give other couples a bad name. On the one hand, two people obviously deeply in love is very sweet. I've been there. It felt great. On the other hand, frottage in the middle of Sainsbury's, completely oblivious to what's going on around you, induces a very specific gut reaction. **Yuk!** Pull yourself together. And pull your top down.

Some couples bring it on themselves. Cutie-pie and Cuddle-buns are asking for it – at least they are if they start using pet names in company. Think how bad it gets around Valentine's Day. The world may be bathed in sunshine and rainbows, but pet names come out in force. It's hideous.

There's clearly a contradiction going on here: many couples love pet names. In my family, two pet names in frequent use are Ploppy Pants and Dickle Dackleton. (Don't ask.) But while the names *we* use are acceptable, all others make us want to curl up and die. Despite our own personal crimes of inanity, it still makes most of us cringe to hear 'cherub' talk to 'my sweetness'.

My mate Alicia, for instance, is very happily married but her sister Charlotte is newly in love and she and her man (Alex) can't keep their hands off each other. They come round to dinner and Charlotte perches on Alex's lap. It's not like Alicia doesn't have enough chairs. If they all go out to the pub together, Charlotte throws a major strop if she can't sit next to Alex – not being able to touch him makes her desperately unhappy, she announces stridently. And, to make things even worse, he addresses her as 'kitten' while she calls him 'sausage'. She's not a cat, she's a fully-grown woman, Alicia wants to scream. And how can a man be called after . . . actually, don't answer that. It's driving Alicia to distraction. She just wants to lock them together in a bedroom for a week and tell them to get it out of their systems. Why does an otherwise normal woman's brain go to seed just because she's fallen in love? It's just embarrassing.

Private pet names can speak volumes about a relationship – so make sure you keep them for your private moments. Watch out for that dangerous stage at which they become so familiar that you forget you're using them. Nobody who hears them will forget – and you never know what the names you use will reveal about you. Baby names, apparently, are often part of a subconscious role-play fantasy. Think about that next time you call your big hunky man your little baby boy. Picture him in nappies.

If you're feeling stigmatised by coupledom, take comfort from the fact that the tide does eventually turn. When you're in your twenties, you might get some funny looks if you're happily loved-up – after all, these are meant to be your wild and carefree days when you play the field. But after thirty, the stigma is much greater for those who are still single. That's the irony. If you're single after thirty, people look at you oddly. They start to think that there's something wrong with you. All of which is rubbish, of course.

Perhaps it's a case of the worm turning. After years of being gently mocked by single people, couples see their chance to return fire. Oh dear, in your thirties and still not found yourself a partner? Not so funny now is it? After all, relationships are not easy. Those who have found long-term happiness with another person have probably had to work at it and are to be congratulated and celebrated, not mocked. Not even if they're called Puppy and Sex Chops. Well, not much at least.

TO SEE OR NOT TO SEE?

How often do you see your new love? Three times a week? Weekends? Every day? What's normal?

There is no such thing as normal, so stop worrying!

Some say that love is a game, and it's sad but true that The Game Of Love might mean playing hard to get, holding back, or not showing your true feelings. Of course if you've been concentrating on this book you'll know by now that being less than honest is a mistake – as is playing games – but you might have been skim-reading so I'll have to make the point again (*sigh*!).

The trick is to be honest about what you want, while reading your new partner's feelings as closely as you can. If you say 'let's meet up tomorrow' and he/she announces they're busy till a week on Wednesday, for example, you can assume that they're not ready for a really intense relationship right now.

I know it's easier to give the impression that you're not too bothered about when you next meet up – there's no fear of looking too keen – but be brave! Be honest! You'll get nowhere otherwise. Standoffishness is a bad sign – and severely contagious – so if you think you and Mr/Ms Hotpants might have a good thing going then don't be backward about coming forward. Being super-keen might be intimidating, but at least it's honest. Think about it from Mr/Ms Hotpants's point of view. You're clearly interested, and that's a good thing, surely?

When a relationship is really good, you skip the games. You see each other with a regularity that suits both of you. When I first started seeing my boyfriend, we very quickly started seeing each other pretty much every day. After a while I needed to recover my own life and spend a few days apart. It wasn't a problem, but it did take discipline. Weighing up whether to stay in bed with him or to go out to the gym was a tough decision. And either way it was exhausting.

It's a hard truth but you will get a little bit sick of each other. No matter how much you love each other, there will come that time when – perhaps just for an hour – you'll want to turn around and for them *not* to be there. It might sound unlikely. It might sound terribly unromantic. But I'm telling you it's true.

Over-kill is the kiss of death

In short, don't give up your individual identities. And above all, lighten up.

- ♥ You suddenly can't bear to be out of your beloved's presence? Don't beat yourself up about it. That's love.

- ♥ You desperately need some time by yourself? Don't worry about it. That's love too.

- ♥ You need a break for an evening? Fine.

- ♥ You said goodbye two minutes ago and you want to see him or her again already? Fine too.

Whatever feels right. Listen to your heart: if it says seven days a week, go for it. And if it says, for crying out loud, go to the bathroom on your own just once, then do that. A good relationship won't mind one bit either way.

GOING STEADY

I admit it, 'going steady' is a terrible Americanism and I probably deserve to be shot for even thinking about using it, but at least I kept away from 'Let's be exclusive'. Yuk. But we stiff-upper-lipped British don't really have a suitable turn of phrase for that fine line you cross between dating and something that could be marriage material. Forget fine lines, it's a terrifying leap!

Before I met my boyfriend I had been single for well over six months – and I was loving it! I was socialising loads, keeping fit, studying, working hard. I liked being in total control. I didn't have to worry about someone else's needs, deal with anyone's changing moods, fit around some man's complicated life. And I simply couldn't imagine how I would ever meet another man with whom it would work out. I had this totally packed schedule from Monday to Sunday, and there was no way I'd be able to work a man into it.

- ♥ Monday night? Sorry, riding class

- ♥ Tuesday? I'm working

- ♥ Wednesday night? That's gym night

- ♥ Thursday? Working again, sorry

- ♥ How about Friday then? Always go out for a bite to eat with my girlfriends Fridays

- ♥ Saturday? Going to a dinner party

- ♥ Sunday then? Back in the gym again

. . . and so on.

My diary was at an all-time height of busy-ness. There was definitely no room for a Special Someone. Impossible. I'd be single for the rest of my life. But the rest of my life would, at least, be very active. I might not have someone to take home to mother, but I'd be very flexible and have muscles the size of houses. And then what about my dog? I could never fall for a man who didn't love my dog. And, seriously, the dog came first. How likely was I to find a man who liked my dog that much?

As it turned out, I met my boyfriend while out walking my dog (amazing what you can find in parks these days). He was out walking his dog too. The dogs got to know each other and so did we. So that, at least, was the dog problem sorted. It was also an interest we immediately had in common. An easy way of spending time together. It might have been a shared interest in cinema (admittedly not so great for conversation) or cars (especially back seats), or whatever. With us it happened to be dogs. But the dogs made it clear to me that it is quite possible for two lives to merge.

Making allowances

The point is that your lives automatically adjust, and you cope. Perhaps you stop going for a jog quite so often, deciding to grow fat together, or you go to the pub six nights a week instead of seven, but it's very rarely something you notice. It's pretty simple. Or at least it should be. And if you're really having to sit down and weigh up whether or you should go to the gym for the tenth time that week, or whether you should see your partner, then either:

- ♥ you are addicted to exercise and need help

- ♥ there's someone you fancy at the gym OR

- ♥ your partner isn't the right person for you

But merging your lives requires a bit of give and take. Be open to new ideas – even if they fill you with complete and utter horror. Give them a go, at least once.

My boyfriend is a keen cyclist and suggested that I buy a bike and we go riding. It was the last thing I wanted to do. But he persisted and I found myself in a strop and on a bike. And actually, once we got going and I stopped sulking, I loved it. It was much the same with camping. He might have been a lover of nature, but I was a lover of domestic appliances. But it turned out that I rather liked camping. Not entirely, mind, but we found an acceptable compromise. If we go away for a long weekend, we spend one night close to nature in the tent. And the other close to civilisation in a very comfortable hotel.

So it's crucial to get used to each other's little habits. My boyfriend, for instance, needs a cup of coffee every morning before he does anything at all. It's simply essential. He and his Blend 37 are inseparable.

Toothbrush traumas

I'm a pink toothbrush, you're a blue toothbrush . . .
but how did we end up in the same mug?

The big toothbrush issue is scary. Have you noticed that when friends are trying to work out how serious you and your new partner are, they don't ask 'Do you talk about love?' or 'Have you met his/her parents?' – they ask 'Does he/she have a toothbrush at your house?'. And the toothbrush thing says it all. For ages it *really* bugged me that my boyfriend used my toothbrush when he stayed over at my house. But both of us would have thought that leaving a toothbrush at my place was somehow a bit too . . . well, forward.

When he finally took that giant leap and bought a blue toothbrush to come and set up house with my pink one, it forced a kind of reappraisal of what the relationship was. It's a bit tricky to carry on pretending you're just two people who happen to get on very well, spend a lot of time together and have fantastic sex if your belongings are making friends. You're clearly planning to make the sleepover a regular thing. So it wasn't long before a few other toiletries, some clean underwear and an emergency T-shirt moved in as well. Inch by inch, his things started to find a permanent living place in my home just as, I noticed, some of my stuff had started to mysteriously appear at his: underwear left in the washing basket is a little sign of a Big Commitment!

SEX GETS IN THE WAY

There is a famous line in *When Harry Met Sally* when the two lead characters are discussing whether men and women can just be friends. Sally says that of course they can. But Harry says that it's impossible because 'the sex part always gets in the way'.

I tend to side with Sally. It *is* possible to have close friends of the opposite sex – but once you're into Big Commitment country, make sure your partner is introduced to them. I'm very territorial when it comes to my boyfriend. I tend to want to spray him with scent before he goes out to meet a female friend – and that's not scent so that he smells nice, that's *my* scent so that the woman in question knows to Keep Her Hands Off.

But I'm completely happy with the situation – there's not even any spraying – if I'm introduced to her first. It stops all sorts of ridiculous imaginings. You find out, for instance, that she is a lovely person (that's why your boyfriend likes her –

you might have more cause to worry if she wasn't), and that, despite your nightmares, she isn't a six-foot blonde with pneumatic boobs and a blinding smile. She's five-foot-ten at best.

I have a friend (Ellie) who spent her first six months with her boyfriend, Dan, insanely jealous of his ex-girlfriend – who she'd never met. And this wasn't an ex-girlfriend who he'd proposed marriage to, or nearly lived with, or declared undying love to. They'd only snogged a few times, but she was the one directly preceding Ellie so Ellie got paranoid. As it happened, Dan didn't really see much of the ex-girlfriend (Annabelle) for the first six months of his relationship with Ellie, but when he did finally get round to seeing her, he very sensibly invited Ellie along. They met up with a whole group of friends – which should have made the whole thing very relaxed and comfortable – but Annabelle turned up about an hour and a half after everyone else, and Ellie unfortunately took advantage of the time to sink serious quantities of alcohol. By the time Annabelle arrived, Ellie had drunk at least a bottle of wine and was beginning to lose the plot. Annabelle is, admittedly, stunningly beautiful – very slim, gamine, blonde hair in a chic elfish cut – and extremely nice, but it probably wasn't necessary for Ellie to lean drunkenly over to Dan and, in a very loud stage whisper, say 'You didn't tell me she was pretty. You bastard.' Dan, hugely embarrassed, told Ellie to pull herself together, so she turned to her best friend and started a loud commentary. 'Bitch,' she hissed drunkenly. 'I bet she's really stupid. People who look like that usually are. And Dan said she was a terrible snog anyway. Apparently she's about as exciting as a potato.' Her best friend tried to shut her up, but Ellie was on a roll. 'And look at her piggy eyes,' she continued. 'Definitely untrustworthy. And she looks anorexic to me. I'd have thought she's probably mentally defective.' Shortly after this announcement, Ellie had to be escorted home. She was very lucky that both Annabelle and Dan were very understanding, but she does of course now have to live with having the piss taken on a very regular basis.

But, Ellie's experience aside, introducing your new sweetheart to the old sweethearts you're in contact with – and to your friends generally, is a good idea. It's only when meetings are clandestine that it all starts to get worrying. No secrets – that's the rule. But there's also another important truth here: you have to spend time apart – alone and with your own friends. It allows you to see the wood for the trees.

When you're too close to someone too much of the time, you begin to forget what it was about them that you fell in love with. They become part of the furniture. You might even forget to fancy them. So if your partner suggests an evening apart, don't throw a guilt trip. I've tried it. It doesn't work.

He might be a bit of a goody-goody, but Sting has some wise words: 'If you love somebody, set them free'. Shakespeare it isn't, but many a true word is said in pop – not counting Steps.

HOME TURF

Getting close means getting very familiar each other's homes. And homes are sensitive places. Don't underestimate the territorial instinct! However much your new girl/boyfriend loves you, they may not want their furniture rearranged.

My friend Louise started seeing this guy, Phil, who was anally tidy. Phil's home was a vision of organisation. Books and CDs formed neat rows. Beds were made. Clothes were hung. Shoes were boxed and stacked. The washing machine was always busy. Louise also had a place for everything. It was called her flat. Everything could go everywhere. It was allowed to roam free. She never knew where anything was and it took her at least half an hour just to get out through her front door. But that's the way she liked it. If the washing-up went undone for weeks, well, it was her washing-up and she could do what she wanted with it.

To Phil, dead takeaway cartons belonged in the bin. To Louise they belonged wherever they landed. It would take the EC Compromise mountain to make a home for both of them. Whenever she stayed with him, she'd only have to turn her back for a moment to find that all her stuff – which she naturally spread over as wide a surface as possible, as though to survey all her worldly goods – had been tidied away, as though he was trying to suggest that it was time for her to leave.

Whenever he stayed at her place, he had to overcome the overwhelming desire to tidy up. Most people would be grateful for a free cleaner but she didn't want her things touched – they were her things and she wanted them where they were. Even if she wasn't quite sure where that was. He had to practice deep-breathing and develop a kind of untidiness-blindness to allow him to cope with it all. You might imagine that they'd never get along. But they're still together two years on. Mind you, they don't live together . . .

There's a certain protocol to getting close to someone – extenuating circumstances such as nightmare flat-mates, living next to the M4 or blocked sewers in high summer aside, the time you spend at each other's place should be pretty evenly split.

I have to confess that this is really a case of do as I say, not as I do as I've always preferred to stay at mine rather than at my boyfriend's. I offer up my dog as my defence – every time I stayed away overnight I'd ache with pangs of guilt at having abandoned her – but generally I think it's a good idea for women to spend their fair share of time at the man's place. Harking back to my Alpha Male theory, this allows the man to feel in control in his own environment. Even if he isn't.

Environmental problems

Of course, girls, you can't expect to have all your essential bits and bobs around you to begin with – moisturiser, night cream, tampons, eye gel, volumizing spray and cotton buds might have to wait a while. And it will be a few weeks before you'll be able to indulge in your day-long bathing ritual without upsetting someone. Accept that it will take some time to adjust to his particular tastes – or lack of them. If he's the standard man (and forgive me for assuming such a thing exists – I know yours is Special), you'll have to expect at least most of the following:

♥ a distinct lack of plants or flowers

♥ an endless laundry pile – around the laundry bin. Men are genetically incapable of taking the lid off and putting their dirty washing in the bin. For them, the laundry bin is just a general marker for the area of floor to be used for washing

♥ a random selection of sticky foams and dust-encrusted pots in the bathroom, none of which seem to have any purpose

♥ the foams and pots will of course make it impossible to find the tooth-paste cap that he's left off

♥ the loo paper is always running out – after all, he doesn't need it as much as you do

♥ fabric conditioner doesn't exist in this environment. It's just a gimmick, isn't it?

♥ bare walls – there won't be any pictures up, except perhaps the odd tasteful (not!) poster of Pamela Anderson. And any pictures there are definitely won't be in frames – except for the odd clipframe his mum gave him as a housewarming present

♥ just accept that there won't be a mirror at the right height for you to do your make-up. In fact you're lucky if there's a mirror at all

♥ in the corner of the bedroom, there will be a stack of

weights gathering dust. And yes, they're just waiting to trip you up

But don't get smug! There's a lot of female peculiarities that men have to endure:

♥ the naff teddy-bear collection that hides the bed. Anything up to four bears or fluffy toys is acceptable. More – or a number of china dolls – is getting worrying

♥ frilly things like valances that don't appear to have any proper function

♥ strange knickknacks cluttering up shelves – and she can't get rid of that strange wooden hedgehog that no one likes because her aunt gave it to her when she was nine

♥ the fridge will be full of mouldering bags of lettuce that she buys when she's on a health kick but never eats because she gets side-tracked by popcorn and pasta

♥ a system for the alignment of shampoo bottles

♥ light bulbs/plugs/electrical appliances that don't work. It's not that she can't fix them, I should point out, it's that she doesn't feel like it. Girls are far more likely to let something broken sit there and become simply decorative.

♥ the female flat is a fire hazard, due to our predilection for candles. Of course we tend to have more than we could possibly ever light at once, but we'll give it a try

♥ getting dressed in the morning is a complicated business which involves trying on at least half a dozen outfits and littering them around the room as we reject them.

There's just not time to put them away.

♥ dead flowers – every so often we'll buy some lovely flowers to brighten up the flat. The problem is that when they die, we may not notice. In our *minds* they still look lovely. Until that water starts to smell . . .

It may all take some getting used to. This really is the suck it and see stage. Whether he rinses the washing-up says a lot about a man. Whether she can decorate in anything other than pastel colours says a lot about a woman. But bear in mind that tidying up for someone won't make them tidy. It will just make them cross. Some people need clutter. Other people need a bottle of Dettol close to hand at all times.

Making a few adjustments
It's all terribly tempting – you just know your way of living is better than his/hers – but bide your time before introducing your own touches. It should be at least two months before you attempt anything as daring as buying a bumper-pack of bath-salts and leaving them in his bathroom. And it should be twice that before you start giving your boyfriend's home a feminine edge: putting up curtains, hoovering, things like that. This is what is known as making a statement. It's a declaration of intent. And that declaration is: this house must change.

A woman who dives into a man's house with a colour chart in her back pocket is not doing him, or the relationship, any favours. It's less a case of slowly slowly catchy monkey as slowly slowly painty wallsy. But avoid setting too many precedents about particular roles: the one who does all the cleaning, the one who does all the cooking, the one who makes the bed or the morning cup of tea. Keep it flexible. A few months down the line, you'll appreciate the fact that you're not designated floor-mopper.

One last thing. Being invited to spend time over at someone else's house is a sign of trust. Don't abuse it. You may have opportunities thrust in your face on a weekly basis, but don't go poking around in your new partner's private belongings. Don't go rooting through desk drawers or reading letters, however much you want to know about his ex. It's none of your business. Besides, you may end up finding something you might not be ready to find. A marriage certificate, for instance. Not so amusing then, is it?

THE BIG NAG

Two conclusions from the McCall observatory of life:

♥ Men sulk.

♥ But women nag.

And, sorry to pick on you, girls, but nagging is **bad bad bad**. It does not work. Is that clear?

Of course making an appointment to discuss what's pissing you off is not only depressingly anal but also just asking for trouble, so the trick is to create an atmosphere in which both partners know that they can catch their beloved for five minutes and tell him or her what's upsetting them. It's awkward at first. It feels a bit like you're in a counselling session. 'My name's Davina and I am sick of you leaving the toilet seat up.' But it does get easier. And, inevitably, you'd never guess which of your peculiar quirks drive the love of your life to distraction. For instance, my boyfriend hated the way I always left the loo roll dangling down to the floor. It didn't get in his way. It didn't make him unable to work or keep him awake at night. It was just something I did that he couldn't stand. Fair enough.

Similarly, he had a habit of switching on the Playstation first thing in the morning. Which would have been fine had it not been in the bedroom and I was still sleeping. Solution: I told him so and now he either waits until I'm awake to start blowing things up, or takes the console downstairs. Simple.

In my experience, the more you love someone, the less these little things become a big issue anyway – you don't make a scene over the washing-up because you don't pick fights with someone you love. And let's face it – it's rare that anyone finds everything they ever wanted in one person. It's a bit like pick'n'mix. Girls can expect any four of the following six options in a man:

- ♥ hard body
- ♥ wit and charm
- ♥ brilliant sense of humour
- ♥ own hair
- ♥ intelligence
- ♥ ability to wash

While men can expect a girlfriend to have four of the following:

- ♥ Elle Macpherson's physique

- ♥ Intelligence
- ♥ The ability to get through the day without Prozac
- ♥ silicone
- ♥ a sense of humour
- ♥ tolerance of your mates

But you can't have them all. It's not easy to drop two, is it? But you might just have to live with it. That way progress (and Happily Ever After) lies.

BATHROOM HABITS

Some unpleasant thoughts

I know your body has been transformed from something you inhabit into an erotic plaything for your new lover. You are A Love God (or Goddess), but at some point you're going to have to face the fact that you poo. So is your lover. There's no escaping it.

Basically, it's OK to leave the bathroom door ajar about one month after you've first had sex. It's really too late to bother about bodily functions that are less than endearing. You've been examined from all angles. They've seen bits of your body that you've never seen. Feeling embarrassed at this point is most definitely closing the bathroom door after the horse has bolted. Quite what a horse was doing in the bathroom is something I think you need to keep to yourselves.

But you understand the mixed metaphor. It doesn't take

long to explode the romantic myth that bodies are naturally clean, tidy, efficient and considerate. And anyone who is still shocked that the most beautiful man or woman in the world does any of the following:

♥ pees

♥ farts

♥ belches

♥ picks their nose

♥ adjusts themselves (more a male thing this, admittedly)

♥ scratches their bottom

♥ has to wipe it

♥ using his or her own hands

♥ and then sometimes doesn't even wash them . . .

should probably consult a psychiatrist. Your lover might have an angelic face, but he or she is *not* an angel.

Farting in particular seems to be a male thing. They find it funny. And there's some bizarre, deep-seated need to make a big show of it – telling you it's on its way, and then cracking a joke about it afterwards, just in case it had escaped your attention. I have to say that, personally, I have no great problem with farting – with my partner farting, that is. I have always tried to be very ladylike. I won't lie and say that I've never farted, nor use some genteel euphemism (ladies don't sweat, they perspire; and they don't fart, they exhale from below). But I can say that I try not to fart in public. For me, bottom belches are something that, if at all possible, should only be let out behind closed (and well-insulated) doors. And I even have a dog to blame.

But I know lots of women who are repulsed by men farting, especially when it creates that oven effect under the duvet. I was once woken from the deepest sleep by the terrific smell that my boyfriend's nocturnal emissions had created. He, of course, slept right through it, while I was forced awake to watch the flowers wilt and the wallpaper start to peel off. It wasn't the silent but deadly kind – a stealth fart. It was worse. Loud and deadly.

The Beauty Myth

On the whole, however, it's best if a couple – no matter how close they are – attempt to tame their bodily behaviour when in each other's company. You both know your body does unpleasant-sounding, unpleasant-smelling things, but it's not necessary to make a feature of it. Try to maintain some mystique. Of course he knows your arm-pits aren't naturally hairless. But it preserves some sense of excitement if he doesn't get to see you shaving them.

There are some exceptions. If the woman is shaving in the bath and he needs to pee, then the mystery has to be dropped momentarily. Don't make him stand outside clutching his crotch – or worse, find somewhere else to relieve himself – just because you're having a depilatory session. But don't start parading the fact that you wax your legs or bleach your 'tache. Sure, a 'tache on a woman is not a good look. But the fact that you deal with this issue is something to keep to yourself. Picking at spots is a similarly bad move. It's lovely that both of you feel comfortable enough to do this, but it isn't advisable in the long run.

There's a point when too much information becomes counter-productive.

The ideal is to create the effect without revealing the effort. Some things should just remain unspoken. If he disappears into the bathroom with the paper and doesn't return for half an hour, you probably know what he's been doing in there but try not to think about it too hard. You may think he has a cute bottom, but this could give your thoughts on it a whole new angle.

While we're on the subject, I should perhaps put in a quick word about what goes on at the other end. Shovelling the food in like there's no tomorrow, noisy chomping or eating with your mouth open need to be stamped on very quickly. Unless your partner is willing to eat behind a closed bathroom door, then a compromise needs to be met on such necessarily public activities. And that compromise is doing it **my way**: steadily, quietly, with your mouth shut.

But I digress. While women need to shave their bikini lines alone, a lot of women love watching men indulge in their own beauty routines. Watching a man shave is often a real turn-on for women, perhaps because it's necessarily such a manly thing to do (spot the double standard: women have to simply appear polished and hairless, without the effort). There is a question of degree here though. There are things you can watch the man in your life do which will make him seem even more irresistible. Then there are those things you really shouldn't know about. A friend of mine was once absolutely horrified to discover that she and her new boyfriend used the same kind of moisturiser. While it was nice to know he looked after his skin, using Ponds' No-Shine Moisturiser was going a bit far. Here's a quick guide to what you should be allowed to see your man do:

Shaving:	fine
A bit of moisturiser:	good
Tinted moisturiser:	getting questionable
Make-up:	a big no-no
A bit of wax:	fine, as long as applied to hair on head
Dyeing hair:	a big no-no (grey and thinning hair should be accepted with grace)

We girls are now used to – and rather like – the idea of you men taking a bit of care with your appearance. It makes you a bit more tolerant of the eight types of toner and six varieties of make-up remover we find it necessary to keep in the bathroom. However, we still expect you to take much less time in the bathroom than us. I can be in and out of the bathroom, from getting out of bed to getting through the front-door, in 25 minutes. Any man who takes longer than that is starting to lose his masculinity for me. My boyfriend can do it in 24 minutes, so he just about scrapes through.

You see although we might be attracted to the classic 'bit of rough', we are aware that looking like a bit of rough takes as much, if not more, effort than it does to look like you've just stepped from the pages of a fashion magazine. That slightly disarrayed hair, that permanent two-days growth of stubble, that T-shirt that isn't sparkly white but isn't exactly grubby either, all take military planning.

And we like the male model look too, of course, but this is just superficial. Women assume much the same about male models as men do about female models: good to look at, but not a lot going on upstairs. Either that, or full of themselves. There is a well-known and widely accepted theory that very good-looking people have had it so easy all their lives that they haven't had to develop a personality. There's certainly something in this. Having worked as a booker at a top male model agency (dirty work, but someone had to do it), I quickly learned the difference between a beautiful man and an attractive man. Every man who came through the door was gorgeous, on paper at least. Gorgeous, but not necessarily appealing. Go figure.

MAKING THE MOVE

Short of getting married or having babies, moving in together is the biggest statement of commitment you can make.

Don't embark on it lightly!

Moving in means that your relationship is serious with a capital S. And if you haven't realised this in a quiet moment on your own, then you shouldn't be doing it.

Many couples move in with the intention of trying it out, or because it makes sound financial sense. You might think it seems like a nice, friendly or sensible idea and that, if it doesn't work out, you can go back to living separately and keep on seeing each other.

You can't!

Once you've moved in together, you either keep living together or you split up. Forever. There's no going back. This all sounds very heavy. That's because it is. Deal with it.

Moving in is basically a commitment to the future. Some people (invariably the ones not worth bothering about) find it hard to commit to something next week, let alone something as definite as sharing a house or flat indefinitely. If you're a commitment-phobe, then try building up to the idea of the long-term: see if you can manage to book a holiday for, say, four months hence without fainting or waking up in a cold sweat every night. See if you can actually take that holiday without having a breakdown. When you get back, see if you can face the idea of discussing *next* year's holiday. If you can, then you're probably capable of committing to living together. If that's what you want.

Holidays are a particularly good way of finding out whether you'd survive living together, or whether the kitchen knife would become exhibit one in a murder trial. You find out whether you can stand each other 24-hours a day, seven days a week. Even the airport can be a testing place, from missing passports to wilful trolleys. There's many a couple who split up after their first holiday together. If you survive that holiday, you're probably onto a good thing.

Making the decision
But even if you're the most committed couple in the world, moving in – and discussing moving in – is scary, so you might choose to discuss it in the abstract. *If you were to choose to live with someone, where would you like to live?* isn't terribly subtle, I admit, and anyone who can't see where this is ultimately leading probably can't tie their own shoe laces yet. But it breaks the ice.

More importantly, if you're worried about living together, **say so now.** Don't wait until the removal men are halfway up the stairs with the new fridge. Treat it as similarly serious to getting married, and you won't end up feeling trapped. Similarly, if you're the one who's particularly keen on the idea, don't smother your partner with hints. Using lots sentences with the words 'moving' and 'in' in them – *I think I'd probably find that film very MOVING, but I'd rather stay IN tonight or Would you mind helping me in MOVING the wardrobe IN to this space* – won't plant some subconscious idea in your partner's head. It will make them think you've lost the plot.

But if you can get past the hurdles, there are basically three types of moving in together:

♥ Ms Right moving in to Mr Right's place

♥ Mr Right moving in to Ms Right's place

♥ Mr and Ms Right choosing somewhere new together

In an ideal world, the last of these is the best option. It's a shared space from the start, and you can bond over wallpaper paste and pots of paint. But this isn't always practical. And if one of you moves into the other's space, there are quite a few pitfalls waiting to trip you up.

For six years I lived with a boyfriend, paying rent, making decisions about the way the place looked. But I was always bugged by the fact that if we split up (as we did) the place would be his, despite the money and effort I had put into it. I'm sure I paid for that new kettle.

And on top of this, it's inevitable that the environment that one of you created – and was totally happy with – will have to change. The Pamela Anderson and Ducati motorbike posters will have to come down. The doily thing over the spare loo-roll and the dusty pot of long-since-odourless pot pourri will have to go. Your love-nest needs to feel nest-like for both of you. And this can be a real battle.

You'll also have to be prepared for the fact that apparently – a male friend of mine swears by this – women undergo a major personality transplant when they move in with a man. Living by themselves, they're slobs. They may seem tidy on the surface, but it's only because you don't live with them that you don't know about what's hidden under the bed. Or behind the armchair. Or about the cups they had to throw away because they went mouldy. But put them in a flat with a man, and they'll become anally tidy. Obsessive. And they'll want the man in their life (or their flat) to keep up to their bizarre new standards. Don't say I didn't warn you ...

If it makes you feel any better, the first two months are always the hardest. Suddenly, you don't have the luxury of having your own room to escape to. Chances are you won't have a garden shed for the man to retire to do hammer things and talk to his copy of *Loaded,* or a boudoir for the woman to disappear into to paint her nails and talk on the phone. You'll be in each other's company pretty much all the time.

Does that sound great?

Or does that sound terrible?

If it's the former for you both, go for it. Living together can be wonderful. It's certainly working for me. I thought I'd just add that in case I'd put you off the idea!

AND NOW, THE MOST IMPORTANT RULE
OF HAPPY COUPLEDOM:

CARRY ON DATING

Yes of course I'm into monogamy, but if you want your relationship to work it's imperative that you carry on dating. Each other. There's some fantastic advice in a fantastic book, *Still Life With Woodpecker*, which tells us that if you want to make love stay, you have to buy love a big piece of cheesecake. Now I've got you confused. But it's true. It's inevitable that you get used to your partner, so it's easy to get complacent, to fall into a run of the mill, shared routine – cosy nights in with the TV, mutual relief that you don't have to go desperately running round in circles to find something to do on Saturday night. This is a fatal mistake!

The intensity of any new relationship wears off. I know you never believe it when you're at the 'Omigod I can't breathe I'm so excited to see you' stage, but the breathlessness doesn't last forever. This isn't a bad thing because you'd die of exhaustion if it did, but if you slip into being too comfortable, you'll be that boring, bored couple you swore you'd never be before you can say *Antiques Roadshow*.

The thing is, when you live together you can see each other at home, so it can sometimes seem a bit of an effort to go out somewhere. *What's the point in going out to dinner*, you'll argue, *when we can stay here and eat microwaved meals in front of the TV. We're still together, aren't we?* Yes of course you are, but when's the last time you phoned a friend and said *Guess what I did on Saturday night. Me and [insert partner's name] stayed in and watched TV. It was great.* Exactly. It's not exactly an evening to write home about. It's not exciting. And if you only ever do boring things together you'll get bored. It stands to reason.

So think of things you'd both like to do. They don't have to be expensive, they just have to be fun. And if you're still feeling confused, here are a few ideas:

♥ Take your girl/boyfriend out for a meal at a restaurant you know they love.

♥ Arrange to go somewhere you know they really want to go – or just somewhere neither of you have ever been.

♥ Tell them they're not allowed to come home until 7.30, and have a candelit meal ready.

♥ Buy them flowers (this advice is mostly for men, admittedly).

♥ Buy them little presents. They don't have to be big, just appropriate.

♥ It's all just a question of working out what would make the love of your life happy. And if you can't work that out, then they're not the love of your life.

My friend Rachel took her boyfriend Omar to see *Star Wars: Episode One*. That might not sound terribly romantic at first, but the thing is that it was a surprise. And it was at the Odeon in Leicester Square. And Omar is a huge *Star Wars* fan (as I am myself, I must confess) – the defining moment of his childhood was being taken to see the first *Star Wars* film at (you guessed it) the Odeon Leicester Square back in 1977, twenty-two years earlier. He'd also seen *Return of the Jedi* and *The Empire Strikes Back* at the Odeon Leicester Square first time round. Add to all this the fact that he was desperately excited about *Episode One* and Rachel got tickets for the first night it was released in the UK, and you'll be starting to understand what a fantastic present it was. She arranged to meet him at Leicester Square tube station and they went for a quick Chinese. Then they strolled past the Odeon, and as Omar looked jealously at all the people going into the cinema, Rachel produced the tickets. He was utterly gobsmacked. And utterly touched. It was the perfect present for him.

A bit less romantic – and even a bit businesslike perhaps – is my friend Jessica's arrangement with her partner.

Each week, Jessica and her boyfriend take turns to arrange an outing. It's the organiser's responsibility to find something that will interest both of them, to book it if necessary and make all of the arrangements. The organisee has to go along on this outing no **matter what**! Even if they're not entirely sure they're into the idea. This way, they both get to experience new things and there's always something new to talk about. Believe me, waking up with a massive hangover at one o'clock on a Sunday afternoon, only to be told that you'll be hang-gliding in a couple of hours gets you talking. Mostly trying to talk your partner out of it, but go with the flow. And take a parachute.

Jessica's system might sound a bit overly-organised, but what the hell, it works. And if you're on a rescue mission for your relationship (or simply want to improve it), then you just want something that's effective. Sometimes you just need one big injection of fun to get things going again – like my mate Andy.

> Andy and his wife have a little (and adorable) baby so, naturally, any nocturnal activities more exciting than getting up four times a night to change nappies is not a likely prospect. With little or no time for each other, the relationship looked to be on rocky ground. But they managed to arrange to go away for one weekend together without the baby and it completely changed everything. That time together, mostly spent in bed together – asleep, admittedly, but at least without interruption – gave them both a new and improved outlook on their relationship. They returned to the baby doting parents – and doting lovers – once more.

But even if you're not in such an emergency situation, we all tend to be frantically busy these days so organise to see your loved one – just as if it was a new relationship. Don't go asking all your friends if they think he likes you and get all nervous about whether he'll turn you down, but make a date for Friday night and stick to it. If a friend calls you up and asks if they want to go out, tell them you're busy. Don't call your partner and tell them you got a better offer. It won't make them feel special.

Keep dating. That, after all, is what it's all about.

Don't Leave Me This Way

OR

Splitting up

Are you sitting down? Do you have a large glass of brandy to hand? You're not holding a cup containing any hot liquids are you? Good. Then here's the bad news.

Breaking up is hard to do.

It doesn't matter whether you're young or old, black or white, gay or straight. Climbing out of the pool of love is as hard as diving into it head first when you can't swim. It's painful, unpleasant, unwanted, upsetting, disorientating, depressing, demoralising and . . .

downright BAD.

Take it from me. I've been there. We've all been there. And if by some bizarre quirk of the unusual you haven't (in which case you either have a desperate need for this book, or alternatively no need at all), believe me, someday it will happen to you.

There is a common misunderstanding that breaking up is somehow easier for the breakerupperer than it is for the breakerupperee (that's the one that's dumped, by the way).

This is **wrong wrong wrong**. Sure, the breakerupperer doesn't get a nasty surprise because he or she knows what is to come, but the breakerupperer has been agonising over it for weeks or even months. They've *already* been living with it while the breakerupperee has been living in blissful ignorance. And they're the one who has had to make that very tough decision – the one who has to live with the inevitable *Have I made a mistake?*, *Was it the right thing to do?* circulating slowly but constantly in their head for months to follow.

All this might lead you to think that my sympathy is with the person who has done the chucking. Of course not – **they're all bastards**, as anyone who has been chucked can testify. How dare they! They should be shot at dawn. But before you reach for your AK47, be aware that chucking isn't an easy thing to do. It takes guts. Even if you really hate those guts right now.

REVENGE IS SWEET

It's especially hard for the chucker (OK, so chucker isn't any more graceful than breakerupperer, but at least it's shorter – besides, I'm a TV presenter, whaddaya expect? Poetry?) when the chuckee exacts their revenge. This isn't a question of:

- ❤ throwing paint over the bonnet of the ex's car

- ❤ cutting the sleeves off all of their suits/dresses

- ❤ telling everyone they have a bit of a problem "you know, down there"

- ❤ sending obscene stories to their boss every week for the next year

It is, rather, a question of turning from the ugly duckling (OK, so ugly's over-stating it, but you could do with a holiday and a trip to the gym, couldn't you?) into a beautiful white swan. And this transformation *always* happens because the first reaction to being dumped is to opt for a major make-over. To re-invent yourself. So: new clothes, losing that extra stone, a better paid job, busier social scene, constant invitations to fabulous parties with very glamorous people, a suddenly-discovered skill as a cordon-bleu chef, new career as a best-selling novelist and film star, hours on sun-beds, thousands of pounds on emulsions and lotions, a haircut, a massage and a whole new you. All within the first fortnight – when the chucker still isn't quite sure that he or she has done the right thing. *Here I am, baby,* you're saying – *you surely gone done the WRONG THING. And now it's too late.*

I learned this lesson at the tender age of nineteen. After a one and a half year relationship, I was dumped over the phone (a heinous crime – see below). In a week I had miraculously metamorphosed from needy teen to glamorous trendy (like the young Joan Collins, I liked to think), stopped biting my nails and one month later I had a new boyfriend – making sure my ex knew about it. And whaddaya know? Boyfriend No.1 was desperate to get me back. It was beautiful.

Did I laugh in his face?

Did I tell him *you're too late, mate*?

**Did I turn haughtily and silently around
and walk away?**

Did I heck. I dumped Boyfriend No.2 and went back to No.1. That taught him, I thought. What an idiot! But, my foolishness aside, the point stands that the best revenge is to better yourself, for you and nobody else.

CUTTING YOUR LOSSES

There are a couple of golden rules:

1. **If a new relationship is wrong for you, get out IMMEDIATELY.**
   Because the longer you are in a relationship, the more difficult it becomes to say bye bye. You become part of each other's lives – sharing mates, a diary and a toothbrush, leaving pants under each other's beds – and cutting ties when you're this involved is mucho bad news. And if you live together – eeek! – it's very bad news indeed. But . . .

2. **It's never too late to get out of a bad relationship. NEVER.**
   There is NO POINT WHATSOEVER (have I made myself clear?) spending any more time on something that isn't working. Even if:

   ♥ you've worked at it so long you can't let all that effort go to waste

   ♥ you've made plans (and paid for them) up to and including the year 2004

   ♥ your boy/girlfriend says they can't live without you

   ♥ you're getting married tomorrow

It's still not too late to leave. This is **your** life, and you're never responsible for someone else's. So eventually you have to have the courage of your lack of convictions and **Get Out**. Of course it ain't easy, it's definitely not pretty and you can bet your life savings it won't be fun, but it *will* be worth it.

I have this nasty habit of attempting to squeeze every last drop of life out of a relationship when it's pretty much at its end of its natural life, even if I know deep down (and I mean *really* deep down, where you don't often want to look) that it really is over and we're just treading water. It's a terrible thing to do. Learn from my mistakes!

PATIENCE IS A VIRTUE

But you really do have to look *deep* down before making that decision to end a relationship. Personally, it's my worst nightmare that I'm in a fundamentally good relationship, but I blow it by pulling the plug because I'm having a bad day, or because it wasn't quite 100% perfect, or because he'd stopped buying me chocolates – only to realise that I was on to a good thing after I've irretrievably fouled the whole thing up.

So if it's a character issue – one of those quirky aspects of your partner's personality that you once loved but which now strikes you as downright irritating, then you have to decide whether:

- ❤ you're just being picky

- ❤ it's something you simply can't live with OR

- ❤ you're a pot calling the kettle black

I once went out with a hippie type of guy. His laid-back attitude to life and general inability to wash struck me as immensely attractive. Well, they did to start with. He was smart, interesting and a good laugh, but – as you'll probably realise, now you know me quite well – at the end of the day I was no hippie. The spark that drew us together became a fuel for fights. All those things I'd found so cute started to seem completely and utterly so revolting. Ugh! Strange how love works . . .

That's why I'm now such a fan of the two-month rule. If I'd followed the two-month rule I'd have known him so much better before we got together, that we might not have got together at all. We might have ended up friends – which is what we should have been. Instead, both ended up on the scrap-heap.

A friend of mine – yes, Jenny again – met a policeman through her work. Her office was burgled and he came round to investigate. So, they got talking and started eyeing each other up (not very professional in the circumstances, but there you have it) and, well you know how it is – and how *she* is. He took down her particulars, showed her his truncheon and a couple of weeks later he called her up on the pretence that he was just updating her with how the investigation was going. Not wishing to appear too keen, my friend responded in kind by sending him a Valentine's card. He rang with 'an update' again and, before you could say 'you have the right to remain silent' (and she wasn't) they were at it.

All was going well. He liked her a lot. She liked him a lot (she'd have preferred a soldier, but a policeman's uniform still did something for her), but then something very wrong happened. He turned out to be not the finest example of the British bobby. First he got a cheap car for her, which turned out to be a stolen car that had been recovered and then accidentally not returned, and from there on it just got worse. Mr Corruption was working overtime. Suffice it to say that this ruined it all for her. She loved everything except his dishonesty. It wasn't something that she could overlook just because everything else was great. So that was the end of that.

FIRST HURDLES

Large-scale extortion on the part of an officer of the law is a bit difficult to overlook. However, small problems, those cracks that appear from time to time in the fine china of love, can usually be worked through and stuck back together. But, unfortunately, small cracks can also develop into gaping great big chasms. These cannot be worked through together. They have to be worked through apart. A long way apart.

But basically I reckon that if you've been together for, say, two years, then you pretty much know everything there is to know about each other – the little bathroom habits, the big needs, the desperate hopes – and if you're still together once you know all this, the relationship has legs. Lots of couples seem very quick to give up on their relationship at the first sign of trouble. For my grandmother's generation, who married young and married for life, a blip in the happy chart

– money problems, a difficult child – was just that, even if that blip was two or three years long. What's two or three years in a lifetime with someone who for the other fifty years you'd choose over anyone else on this planet? And while I'm **not** recommending staying with someone who makes your skin crawl, blips will inevitably happen.

After two years that honeymoon period is probably over. The chocs have melted, the flowers are dead, the fluffy bunnies don't make quite so many fluffy bunnies as perhaps they used to. But that's hardly a reason to scratch the whole relationship. If you're prepared to work at it, clearly there's something very good indeed worth salvaging. Admittedly it takes time and effort and patience. And it's bloody hard. But it pays off. Take my word for it. I've been a troubled and troubling child, a mad and bad adolescent, and only in recent years evened out as myself. And, despite growing up as I did, keeping a relationship going is by far the toughest thing I've ever done.

I was out at a friend's party a few nights ago, and it had hit that five o'clock in the morning stage so – naturally – we started talking about relationships. More specifically, we were discussing whether marriage – as a concept – can ever work. There were lots of negative noises until one bloke, Mark, said he definitely thought it could, as long as you went into it on the understanding that it might take a lot of effort from time to time. That sometimes you'll have six months that aren't fun, but if you love each other enough, if you're committed to being together enough, and work at it enough then you'll make it back to Happyville. I sat there nodding sagely, and suddenly realised that everyone else was looking totally surprised – and totally impressed at his level of commitment to his girlfriend. And I found that absolutely terrifying – that they hadn't all realised that relationships work! *It's a fact of life,* I wanted to scream. *Live with it, or live alone*!

I got married and it didn't work out. I'm not bitter about marriage in the slightest. But I know that I want what's right for both me and my partner before I get married again.

MAKING THAT DECISION

According to my dad, a great relationship has, in no particular order:

- ♥ Carnality
- ♥ Friendship
- ♥ Trust
- ♥ Respect

If any one of those things goes, then the relationship is in trouble and needs repairing. You might need a third party to give you a bit of help, and counselling is not something to be sniffed at. But for this to work you also have to know yourself. I've only ever split up with someone – well, I've only ever been the chucker – when things have got so bad that I simply cannot imagine being with them anymore. The idea just seems impossible. All communication has gone. I could hardly even bear to look at them anymore. That's how bad it has to be before I'll concede that the relationship is over. Until that point I'll try everything to get it back on its feet.

And maybe that's a bit extreme. I'll admit that it probably takes me much longer than most people – and longer than is sensible – to realise that the one thing bugging me is in fact an unreconcilable difference. That this is a relationship worth getting out of. If only because being with someone who is only 90% right for you is effectively shutting the door to meeting that person who is 95 or 100% right for you. The trick is working out whether your lover is 90% right or 98% right.

I've got a friend, Melanie, who has this gorgeous, adoring, lovely boyfriend. They've been together for about three years and he loves her to death. And she loves him. The problem is, she can never decide whether he's Mr 90% or Mr 98%. He wants them to move in together, but she sits there and moans (to me, not to him) 'What if I meet someone better the day after we move in together? What if there's someone more perfect for me just around the corner?' Now personally, I think she should just get a grip. If he's not right for her then she should end it. Now. Put him out of his misery. And if he *is* right for her, then she should take that leap. She might enjoy it. Either way, this 'someone perfect round the corner' thing drives me mad. If you thought like that about everything, you'd never be able to hold a job – you'd have to spend all day scouring the *Positions Vacant* pages – and as for deciding what to do on Saturday night? What if you got a better offer just as you'd committed yourself to something? You'd spend your life a jittery mess, never leaving the house for fear of missing something. It drives me mad.

EVERY ONE A WEDDING

When I was younger I used to think of every relationship as part of a journey towards The Big Relationship which would end in marriage and babies and a nice house in the country with toddlers pulling on my apron strings and pigs in the courtyard.

But not yet, thank-you.

But I'm après-thirty now, and although if you haven't hit the big 30 yet you might think I'm stark staring bonkers, now I'm older every relationship is **The One**. Each one is the real thing. Après thirty, each relationship potentially ends in marriage. I know, I know. It sounds mad. I'm too romantic for my own good. But, believe me, it's nothing to do with romance. As a woman, this is simply to do with my **Biological Clock**.

My clock ticking. And it does put enormous pressure on the relationship to succeed. Here's **McCall's ironic rule of relationships:**

♥ The younger you are, the *less* bothered you are about relationships working out and the *easier* they are to come by.

♥ The older you are, the *more* bothered you are about relationships working out and the *harder* it is find one.

Just one of life's little jokes.

There are lots of people who think that a relationship is all about passion. Of course, it is on one level: the horizontal one. But it's not about passion in all things. A good relationship doesn't alternate between tearing each other's clothes off one minute and trying to kill each other the next. Throwing the crockery around does not result in greater understanding. It results in eating out of the tin.

And, let me tell you – as someone who used to be obsessed with passion – tears and hysteria get very tiring after a while. You run out of things to smash. Your voice gets hoarse. And then you realise that being in a relationship that is so good it can look after itself (that's not to say effort isn't always required), is a pretty fine thing. A calm, steady, easy relationship isn't necessarily a dull relationship. So cut the amateur dramatics and, if you're feeling a bit bored:

Do something about it. Get out there and do things!

But anyway, that's enough about avoiding the big KO (that's kiss off, if you're not sure). Let's get on with doing the dirty deed . . .

KILLING THEM SOFTLY

Dumping someone is no fun. Don't ever try to think that it is. Don't ever try to make a joke about it. Don't laugh and don't giggle. **Just don't.**

In fact, dumping is all about don'ts. And here are the crucial ones. Please don't deviate from this list. We want to make this as painless as possible for everyone involved – not just for the dumper:

♥ DON'T dump anyone by phone or by voice-mail, by fax or by e-mail, by DVD or by CD-ROM or any of the other techno-whizz gadgets that mean you don't actually have to speak to anyone face to face. This is a chicken-shit thing to do and is simply unacceptable. Anyone who dumps via these methods deserves a good whipping.

Do as you would be done by.

Don't do with the intention of doing over.

These methods might allow the breakerupperer to have control over the situation, but they just make the breakerupperee feel worthless.

♥ DON'T break up over their kitchen table, or yours. You may well have done other things over this kitchen table and the memory of that might not be entirely appropriate right now.

♥ DO break up face to face and on neutral ground. You need to make sure that it won't totally complicate the breakerupperee's life to have this place contaminated by the inevitable bad feelings you're about to awaken in them. Do it in a pub, for instance. They can always find a new local. It's more complicated to find a new kitchen. There is also a slightly more sneaky reason for choosing a neutral place. Some people react in a very strange way when they get the shove. They lose their marbles momentarily. They might have a screaming fit or try to kill you. But they won't do this in the middle of the Dog and Duck. Well, they probably won't. If they're really mad they'll do it anyway. But at least this way you minimise the risk.

♥ DON'T be seen with your new girl or boyfriend within two miles or two months of the split-up location and time. That's just courtesy.

♥ DON'T leave the door open. Not literally, of course, though if they're really mad, closing it behind you will at least give you a headstart when they come hurtling after you with the bread-knife.

But what I'm getting at is: be definite. After all, this decision should be the result of many long sleepless nights considering every possible way to save the relationship. It's a considered decision. And it should be a final one. If you're splitting up, you're splitting up. You're not seeing how it goes. Or how you feel in a week. Or going away to think about things.

Are you together or not? If not, then not. That's it. Over. Completely. *Comprende?* Anything less simply leaves the chuckee with a chink of hope that will soon become a yawning canyon. It makes the whole nasty event all the more painful. Be honest and kind, but brutal. Don't try to let them down gently. There is no gently.

♥ DON'T labour the point. Keep it short. Don't end up getting into an analysis marathon. It's too easy to be talked out of doing something that isn't nice to do in the first place. Besides, there shouldn't be a lot to say. And the longer the chuck-chat, the more the chucker and the chuckee will feel like a bastard and a schmuck respectively.

If you're not sure quite what your feelings are, I've been told that it's a good idea to write a letter to the chuckee explaining your feelings and reasons. **Don't send it**. But be sure to put it away and read it a few days later. If you still feel the same, then it's time to chuck. Send the letter after you've done the deed to provide fuller explanation. If you don't feel the same, **burn that letter before it falls into the wrong hands**! But if you do send it, you must allow the dumpee to reply. That's just good manners.

♥ DON'T try to explain in detail. This only allows the chuckee the opportunity to explain why things happened, or promise to make things better. A simple *I don't know quite why yet, but I've considered this for a long time and the relationship doesn't feel right to me anymore* is best. It's emotional and, above all, unanswerable. Vague is good. Sometimes that's all you can offer.

♥ DON'T let the dreaded cross-over happen. We all have eyes for others occasionally, no matter how much in love we are. But if you meet someone else who really means something to you (especially after the two-month rule which, although it might be hard to manage when you're single, you should *definitely* stick to if you're in a couple!) then it's time to reassess the relationship you're in. Picture the new love of your life in full. What might they be like in the long-term? Is that wild and crazy attitude to life that you find so attractive right now likely to drive you mad later? Are you rejecting a lifetime of soul-to-soul understanding for a moment (well, hopefully a couple of hours) of fun?

Some people might look like an attractive package, but that's not the same as knowing them. Even if I say so myself, I'm not a bad package: I'm confident, presentable, got a good job . . . but I'm also really really hard work. So, the bottom line is don't start a Relationship No.2 as a safety net to land in when you end Relationship No.1. That's cowardice. Split up first. Besides, I'm sure I'm not alone in finding it hard to trust a man who started seeing me while seeing someone else. Dodgy.

♥ DON'T ever use the following words: "I just don't fancy you anymore". It's cruel and not to be condoned. Besides, have you looked at yourself lately. You're no oil painting . . .

♥ DON'T start blaming anyone. Remember that just as it takes two to tango, it also takes two to want to kill each other. Even where someone's been unfaithful, it's often the relationship – rather than the love-rat – which is at fault. Accept your half of the blame. And be honest. Don't start fobbing them off with those time-honoured (and quite appalling) backing-out phrases. Don't start telling them that they're 'too nice' for you. If that's the case, why are you leaving?

IN SHORT, SPLIT UP RESPECTFULLY.

And if you're still unsure about the routes not to take to let your former beloved know they're out of your life, here are a few more hints:

Sometimes it's just the little things that give you a clue that the relationship is over:

A friend of mine, Richard, got home one day to find that his key no longer fitted in the lock. His girlfriend (sorry, that should be ex-girlfriend) had taken the day off work to get the locks changed. And delivered all his belongings to his parents' house. Of course it probably didn't help that when I saw him looking blue the next day, I dragged him into the nearest coffee shop for a chat.

'What's wrong?' I demanded, unaware of Sarah's defection.

'It's Sarah,' he said. 'It's all over.'

'Rubbish,' I said, determined to cheer him up. 'It can't be. There's bound to be a bit of room for negotiation once you get talking. It's not like she's changed the locks on you.'

I don't think I helped.

The worst dumping story I've ever heard, however, happened to my friend Sophie:

My friend Sophie had the distinct feeling that all was no longer blooming in the garden of love between her and her boyfriend, Adam Bevis. He was a bit of a workaholic and they hadn't been seeing much of each other recently, so she started planning a romantic weekend away to bring the spark back. She booked the hotel, told him to keep the weekend free, and started buying sexy underwear like it was going out of fashion. Then, a few days before the big weekend was due to happen, she got a call from her best friend, Emma, summoning her to an urgent lunch. Sophie, realising that something was up but assuming it was Emma's lovelife they were to discuss, trotted off to Café Rouge for lunch. As soon as she sat down, Emma forced a double gin and tonic down Sophie's throat, held her hand, then thrust a copy of that morning's *Times* under her nose. It was open at the engagements section, and this is what Sophie saw:

> **HANLEY-BEVIS.** Giles and Emily Hanley are happy to announce the engagement of their daughter, Helen Louise, to Adam James Bevis, eldest son of James and Sarah Bevis.

Bastard! That's all I have to say.

AND IF YOU'RE THE CHUCKEE...

There are two ways of dealing with this.

1. **Save face.** Be respectful of how your partner – sorry, your ex-partner – must be feeling right now, what nerve it took to tell you how he or she felt. Have some respect for

yourself and maintain a cool, calm exterior, accepting that emotions are complicated things.

2. Scream the house down!

I go for No.2 every time. Forget being sedate and collected. I've just been dumped! How dare he? Doesn't he know how lucky he is? How there's a list as long as . . . well, pretty long anyway, of men just waiting to fill his shoes? Crying, screaming, pleading, begging and collapsing might not be the most dignified exit, but at least it will leave you both with something to remember when, at a later date and on better terms, you reminisce over what a horrible moment that was.

Remember that there is very little you can do in this situation. You won't change their mind – and if you do, not only do you deserve an Oscar, but you should bear in mind that this is likely to be only a temporary reprieve. A day, week, or month down the line, you'll have to go through it all again. And nobody gets two Oscars for the same performance.

Men and women differ in the ways they deal with being dumped.

Men . . .

💔 Go into denial. They were never dumped – they split up by mutual decision. Or better still, they did the dumping themselves. Even if word gets out that he was the one dumped, you can bet he'll think it was for the best and that it was something he was about to get around to doing himself.

♥ Aim to have another girlfriend within 24 hours. Seven days tops. Ideally she will look nothing like the girl who has just dumped him. If the ex was a quiet brunette who was happiest tucked up in bed (reading, that is), the new girl on the block will be a loud-mouthed blonde with a penchant for dancing on the table. This proves, obviously, that the foolish ex who recently dumped him was clearly not his type anyway.

Alternatively, he'll go out with someone who looks just like you – but who doesn't chew her toe-nails in bed. This move to get a new girlfriend is accompanied a national media and PR campaign to ensure that his ex knows all about it. Ideally he'll want them to meet as soon as possible, preferably while he's snogging the new girl at one of his and his ex's old haunts. But rebound girl never lasts long. He's kidding himself.

♥ Don't talk about it. It's just one of those things, water under the bridge, old news and life goes on. Inside he might well be crying. Outside he's Father Christmas meets Coco the Clown. One big jolly person.

Women . . .

On the other hand have one reaction to being dumped: get all their friends together and tell them everything in the minutest detail, repeating themselves over and over again. They all cry a lot – even those girls who never even met the man, or hadn't realised they were seeing each other – and complete the most deadly, high-precision character assassination known to man (or, rather, not known to man). If the dumpee has never been chucked before they will come to the conclusion that it is a good, character-building experience. They will see something positive in it. They might still want to kill the dumper, but they'll feel stronger for having been put through the dumping.

AFTER THE SPLIT

This is a time for great diplomacy, even if you spend each night sticking needles into small wax dolls. It's best to wait a while before trying to resume any form of communication – not counting letter-bombs and the like.

Quite often, in my experience at least, it's the break-erupperer who ends up calling the breakerupperee first, especially when the former is a bit full of him or herself and expects their ex to ring them up pleading for a second chance. But **please note:** this is not a sign that they've changed their mind so don't get all excited and assume that means they want to get back together with you. All it means is that, in many ways, the split has been as hard for them as it has for you.

So keep your distance for a while, but use this time constructively. If you're going to be miserable, be miserable with some conviction:

- ❤ Wear black

- ❤ Don't eat

- ❤ Powder your face to make yourself look paler

- ❤ Don't sleep for several nights

- ❤ Moan gently all the time

- ❤ Do this for a few days

♥ **And then stop for good**

In short, do whatever you feel is right (and legal) to get it out of your system, but don't make a career out of it. Don't kid yourself that you're super-strong and can handle it. Don't lock up all your emotions until you next see your ex and subsequently fall apart in the middle of Safeways. Be honest with yourself. Talk about it with friends (no problem here for most women), but don't bore them to death with it. It's bad enough that you've just lost one friend. You don't want to lose them all.

A few tips for coping:

♥ Pull yourself together:

♥ Get out of the house.

♥ Don't mope.

♥ Be active.

♥ Take up jogging. But don't do circuits round your ex's house.

♥ Go out clubbing (that's dancing, not assault).

♥ Go fishing. There are plenty of fish in the sea.

♥ Provide your own entertainment. Throw a dinner party. That's my solution. If I'm on my own in this situation I'm in bad company, so I play Hostess for weeks on end. This, I should add, is also a great way of meeting new people – people who might, at a later date, prove to be romantically interesting.

♥ Try to avoid gossip and gossiping. Yes, of course it's interesting to know that his new girlfriend is a Swedish nuclear engineer, artist and part-time catwalk model. But is it good for you to know that she's also loaded? Try not to spend all your time slagging your ex. Not only does this make you look more than a little sad, but it's a waste of energy. Besides, you may – just may – end up together again. I'm not promising anything but it does happen. And when he finds out you've been telling everyone that he eats his own bogies and fancies his sister, he will not be pleased.

♥ Be prepared for the long haul. Don't expect to get over it in a matter of days. Apparently there is some psychological rule of thumb that says it takes one year of grieving over a dead relationship for every two years that it lasted. It certainly took me at least three years to get over my six-year relationship.

♥ Be collected and considered. Don't go all bitter. Bitter is most definitely unattractive. Bitter people are the type who make huge, inaccurate and plainly illogical generalisations about how terrible all men or women are. It's boring. It's wrong. It's dumb. So just don't, OK? Control yourself.

♥ This is a male speciality, but try not to rush into another relationship. Get over the one you've just been shoved out of before diving into another. It's not impossible to meet Mr or Ms Perfect a week and a half after being unceremoniously dumped, but face it – it's unlikely. So make sure you're not using someone to comfort your own ego – that's to say, you're not just on the rebound.

By the same token, don't start out on a world shagathon. This might satisfy certain momentary needs, a quick fix like a giant Mars bar. But, just like too much chocolate too quickly, you'll end up taking part in a head-over-the-toilet-athon. Not nice.

People who have just split up with someone are radioactive. They're vulnerable, prickly, lost – all of which, ironically, is an attractive combination to some people. They radiate a relationship problem. If I was a doctor of emotions, I would prescribe six months of the single life in order to gather your thoughts and reflect on the situation. Take some time to think about what YOU want and:

♥ TRY TO BE HAPPY. This isn't about putting a brave face on the situation, though that's surely better than the damp, crumpled-up face you wear when you're wilfully miserable for months on end. Believe it or not, when you fake happiness, it sometimes starts to become a reality. Call me an old hippie, but it's like visualisation: if you imagine it happening often enough, it will happen. If you imagine yourself with Brad Pitt long enough, you will be with Brad Pitt. No, you're right, visualisation doesn't always work. But sometimes it does, so it's worth a shot.

A FINAL WORD

So much pain, so little gain?

Not exactly.

Dating, going out with someone, being in a relationship, having a partner – call it what you will – can be a wonderful experience that nobody should be without. It's fun, exciting, expanding, improving and part of life. It's the greatest part of many people's lives.

But it's also sometimes very painful. This is the price you pay – and, when you find Mr or Ms Right, the price you will hopefully no longer have to pay. It's work, but it's work that brings its own reward. All the anguish and upsets are worth it in the end, because they get you to where you want to be: with someone you love unconditionally and find utterly irresistible for a long, long time.

Ending a relationship isn't pleasant, of course. But – and I almost forgot this – it does have not one but two great advantages.

1. It means that you are free to enter the world of dating again – and whatever your age, dating is possibly the world's greatest source of fun outside Disneyland

2. You get to start this book again from the very beginning. Wondering how to get a date? Turn to page one . . .

lots of love,
Davina xx